Writing Tides

To Brigitte,

Blessings on the tides
of your life.

Kent Ira Groff

Chautauqua 2009

Writing Tides

Finding Grace and Growth Through Writing

Kent Ira Groff

Abingdon Press
Nashville

WRITING TIDES
FINDING GRACE AND GROWTH THROUGH WRITING

Copyright © 2007 by Abingdon Press.

All rights reserved.

This book is printed on acid-free paper.

Library of Congress Cataloging-in-Publication Data

Groff, Kent Ira.
  Writing tides : the rhythms of grace in writing / Kent Ira Groff.
    p. cm.
  Includes bibliographical references and index.
  ISBN 978-0-687-64265-6 (binding: pbk., adhesive-lay-flat)
  1. Spiritual journals—Authorship. 2. Authorship—Religious aspects—Christianity. 3. Contemplation. 4. Spiritual life—Christianity. I. Title.

  BV4509.5.G697 2007
  248.4'6—dc22

                                                                  2007000385

07 08 09 10 11 12 13 14 15 16—10 9 8 7 6 5 4 3 2 1
MANUFACTURED IN THE UNITED STATES OF AMERICA

C o n t e n t s

Writing Resources

Acknowledgments

I call the people listed here "acknowledgmentors" since I acknowledge each as a mentor in this writing journey: Mark Altschuler, Sue Barley, Marilyn Mathews Bendiksen, Tom Brackett, Todd Carter, Robert Cheung, Donrico Colden, Barbara Nash Flannery, Liz Hallen, Mary Lou Houser, Mary Jean Irion, Patricia Johnson, Crystal Lyde, Stephen Melton, Bro. Anthony Rex, Jordan Pfautz, Keith Wilson, and myriad participants in my writing workshops, retreats, and classes.

I am especially grateful for readers who gave me creative and critical feedback on the draft manuscript: Rich Gelson, Richard Jorgensen, Wanda Schwandt, and Tom Cartwright, plus writer friends in our Inklings group: Keith Beasley-Topliffe, Keith Bitner, and Seth Obetz.

I first met my editor John Kutsko when he was leading a writing seminar in Philadelphia. His generous affirmation and keen direction in specific instances have guided the lively development of the whole.

Always I am thankful for my life companion and wife, Fredrika, and the rhythms of her support for me to engage with passion and at times to withdraw for perspective.

Kent Ira Groff
Denver, Colorado

Orientation

People write all the time: personal to-do lists, memos at work, applications for schools and jobs, minutes of a meeting, reminders to a roommate, lover, or spouse. We send notes to thank, to sympathize, to congratulate, to motivate. We draft letters, e-mails, blogs, and text messages. Many keep a spiritual journal. We compose newsletter articles for business, church, or community groups and essays for professional journals. Elders compile family and personal stories in hopes of linking generations separated by geography, divorce, or culture.

I aim to show how every form of writing—practical notes or analytical essays, fiction or nonfiction, poetry or autobiography—has the potential of calling forth the spiritual dimension that can unlock the treasure of your life's purpose.

During a time when I was getting several writing rejections, two things occurred to me. First, if I write for myself it doesn't matter if it gets rejected. Second, when work or duty demands I write something, if at the end of a day I find myself an inch closer to my own heart and the Heart of the universe, then obligation has morphed into invitation.

I hope you experience the reality of the title, *Writing Tides:* penning your way home to your true self and out into the world's need—the tides of contemplation and communication. It means developing subtle contemplative insights in writing personal reflections and in task-related writing—even if neither sees the light of publication.

A Matter of Life and Death

Writing can be a matter of life and death. Jon flew three thousand miles to his home state to be with his comatose father. The next evening he read his father a note penned by his own twenty-something son. Jon tells how minutes after "hearing" his grandson's words, his father began to breathe slower, ebbing into a peaceful death.

A soldier was killed in the Civil War, but the letter he had penned to his lover survived. Now, through Ken Burns's TV program *The Civil War*, that letter gives life to a still warring world.

Etty Hillesum, killed in Auschwitz at age twenty-nine, wrote in her diary *An Interrupted Life*, "I believe in God. And I want to be right in the thick of what people call 'horror' and still be able to say: Life is beautiful." Incredible. Like Anne Frank's *The Diary of a Young Girl*, each one's writings, conceived in death, continue to bring life.

On the other side, innocent persons, especially among minorities, are wrongly imprisoned or executed by means of a "sentence." Written verdicts can liberate or condemn. Writing is as exhilarating and frightening as Everest.

Like a tsunami, an impulsive letter written from within a deep tide of anger can actually "kill" a relationship. Yet as Abraham Lincoln understood well, the same letter, written but never sent, can prevent or restore a broken relationship.

Here's the unique invitation to everyone who writes for love, labor, or learning—or if you're fortunate, all three. Express your soulful self—whatever the subject—letting your joy or angst surprise you and draw you deeper into your true self and the mystery at the heart of the universe.

Whether you contemplate and communicate concrete facts and figures or imaginative figures of speech, the invitation is the same: to weave a creative *and* critical double thread while presenting your thoughts with integrity. You can follow this spiritual thread running through both informational and inspirational writing—whether in your personal journal or for a published professional journal.

Features: Using This Book

I hope you will not just read *about* writing, but also experience fresh moments of awareness of self, others, and the awesome Presence that permeates the universe with mysterious inklings of love and life. Special features create openings for that to happen.

Reading in solitude. *Writing Tides* integrates writing methods and spiritual practices, the ebb and flow of communication and contemplation. Interactive exercises (at the end of each chapter) and resources (in the back) invite you to delve into life issues to discover a holy calling and meaning in the muddle.

For ease of reading, you may bookmark the notes in the back of the book (listed by chapter and page number) to locate authors and sources cited in the text. You can dig deeper using the bibliography and references in the notes. Note: first names used in stories in the text are not actual names of the persons.

You may periodically find yourself dipping into the contemplative writing exercises while reading along in each chapter's ideas and information, stories, and questions. Or you may use them like an exercise bar for daily or periodic devotions.

Reading in community. Even if you read the book alone, I hope you find yourself sharing bits and pieces of it. Use *Writing Tides* to renew a friendship at a distance, conversing by phone or e-mail. Connecting intentionally with others can add deeper layers of learning. Try meeting with a few other pilgrims who are willing to talk about the texts and texture of their lives. Use the book as a resource to spawn a small group or a series of classes or to plan a retreat.

Create safe, nurturing environments at homes, libraries, campuses, prisons, churches, or continuing education and retreat centers. As an option for any gathering, break into small "Inklings" groups (two to six) to share the exercises; then re-gather with the whole group. Be comfortable with silences, and find some rituals of closure (see resource 3).

Keeping a journal. Journaling is a way of creating markers in your journeying. A journal is a tool for noticing spiritual layers in ordinary experiences; it benefits personal and group life. I will coach you along the way with "props" like the exercises that make good grist for journaling (see resource 1). To write your way home is to connect your own deep passion with the worlds of family, relationships, work, and political life.

Fiction story. Each chapter opens and closes with a story (in *italics*) acting as a bookend to transport you into the writing tides of a wonderstruck child during the first week at the beach—a child who gets surprised every day. The five days form the chapter themes of the book. Now it's time for the child to get her feet wet.

A Child's First Week at the Beach

Meet seven-year-old Marin. Imagine this Kansas child's very first week at the beach. Monday she's all eyes and ears, observing—enthralled by sand, salt, waves, and shells. Tuesday she starts wading—still a bit self-conscious, looking over her shoulder to see if her grandmother thinks she's gone out too far, wonderstruck by waves and sky and smells. Wednesday she's swimming— learning new methods for going out farther for longer stretches, reducing her fear by internalizing skills to navigate unpredictable currents. Thursday she imagines herself all grown up and ready for deep-sea diving— astounded by majestic coral, yet confident because she's learned methods to get back up. Friday she's floating— outside of time, one with the water and carried in the flow.

The process of writing rarely follows such precise stages. Rather symbolic "days" interact with each other. Each day's theme includes the tides of contemplating and communicating, like the single edge of a Möbius strip, ever turning and reappearing, always in process. I invite you to our first reflection exercise—a simple hands-on project of creating your own Möbius strip to represent the tides of contemplation and communication (see exercise 1).

Each stage of writing has the potential for writing into your own heart and the Heart of the universe — and out into the universe of action. Join me as we begin this writing journey, one day at a time.

EXERCISE 1 — *Creating a Möbius Strip*

Named for August Ferdinand Möbius, a German mathematician and astronomer, the strip is

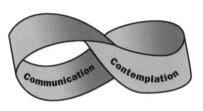

used practically for industrial belts so that the surface wears evenly on "each" side — its one side. You can make a simple Möbius strip: cut a strip of paper (for example 1" x 11"). Lay it flat and write "contemplation" to the left and "communication" to the right. Now loop it, and turn one end over to the reverse side, tape or glue the two ends together. If you rotate it you will see it is a single surface that reappears: alternately the word contemplation will appear on the inside, and communication on the outside — then vice versa. Meditate on how we contemplate and communicate within and without. Try writing any "opposites" on the surface and meditate on the paradoxical nature of life.

Observing—Focus on Awareness

Paying attention in all directions

Monday Morning

Since turning five, when her dad died and her mom remarried, Marin has spent her summers on Grandpa and Gram Panofsky's farm where she'd go skinny dipping and doggy paddling in the pond. Even a required swim course at North Kansas School for Youth could not prepare Marin for a long-promised trip to Gram's friend's apartment near Florida's Miami Beach. Here she is at the ocean her very first day—observing breezes, laughter, sand, clouds, saltwater, seagulls, boats, and people with picnic lunches. One minute she wants to run into the sea, the next she wants to run away. It's too scary for her child-size psyche to think of wading into the waves—let alone jumping into them—yet. Maybe tomorrow. Maybe twenty years from now when she comes back as a marine biologist to contemplate the same stuff from different angles. Today, this child just walks around mesmerized and a bit iffy about everything.

Worthy writing begins by showing up at the shoreline with round-faced innocence. Actually to a child nothing is *un*worthy if you can see, hear, touch, taste, or smell it. Research in any field is about clear-minded observation: being present to *all* the data, mind-boggling facts *and* feelings so incredible you can't find words for them yet.

Blaise Pascal, forerunner of modern computer scientists, was a thinker's thinker. He got so giddy observing some of his higher math calculations that he wrote, "The loneliness of these infinite spaces frightens me." But observing his fears as well as the figures propelled him into contemplation beyond calculation. In scribbled fragments published after his death as *Pensées* — "thoughts" — Pascal is still giving the world spiritual insights that surely rival his mathematical discoveries. Thinking and thanking come from the same Middle English root, *thenken*. Scientific and technical writers, take note.

SLOWLY
GOODLY

I think:
Goodly
things are
happening
slowly.
I thank.

"In-Between" Spaces: Liminal Awareness

The shoreline is *the* place to begin. Did you ever notice how primal revelations in spiritual traditions often occur beside water? Moses and the Hebrew slaves cross the sea of reeds to enter the land of promise. Jesus calls disciples by the seashore, "Follow me!" In risen form Jesus builds a charcoal fire by the sea, saying, "Come and have breakfast." The Buddha spoke of using a raft (spiritual practices) to cross the river into Enlightenment. Depth psychology compares the human unconscious to the ocean.

The outward shoreline corresponds in *space* to the liminal state within each of us. *Limen* in Latin means threshold, the doorway in which the conscious life of thinking and acting meets the storehouse of unconscious knowing and dreaming. Likewise, sunrise and sunset correspond to this inward liminal state in *time*. Mountain summits serve the same purpose in primal societies. Even in our postmodern culture, shorelines and mountaintops still lure us into respite and restoration. Once while at the New Jersey shore, I woke up by surprise at 4:30 a.m. Sitting on a rock, a stranger and I watched in silence as the sun arose sliver by sliver, until its colossal arc, magnified by the ocean mist, illuminated the entire sky. I wager the effects of such environments mysteriously tap open the window of the soul—one's true self—no matter what subject or whether a person is religious, atheist, or agnostic.

Original writing—whether highly analytical or intensely spiritual—taps into some threshold of deeper awareness. Such ripe moments often occur in REM (rapid eye movement) sleep or semi-dozing, in meditation or prayer.

The problem in a fast-paced society is not how to produce liminal experiences; it is how to allow time and space to notice what's already there. Writing begins with observing, so awareness is the first layer of our response to what surrounds us. Since our ancestors first learned to speak, then write and read, words have been a way to respond, record, and reflect on lived experiences.

The Tree: Paradigm of Contemplation and Manifestation

How can we cultivate the art of listening beneath the surface of family dynamics, corporate scandals, political angling, global warming and warring, tensions in our bodies?

The most important Hebrew prayer is the *Shema*, named for the first word meaning hear, listen or pay attention — or obey. "Listen, O people of God, the Lord your God is one." Deep listening draws us into loving connection with God, neighbor and self, as Jesus reaffirmed in Mark 12:29. Mindfulness is the term for such contemplative listening in Eastern traditions. *Shema* means attentiveness with one's soul, one's whole being — heart, will, mind, and body. To write of anything significant begins with awareness of its significance for you.

Days pass, years vanish, and we walk sightless among miracles.

—Hebrew prayer

The tree stands as a paradigm of the spiritual life in Judeo-Christian and scores of indigenous traditions. Imagine the upper part of the tree as a *manifestation* of our life of action, bearing fruit in the world, risking stresses of wind and weather. Imagine the root system as the hidden life of *contemplation*, beneath conscious awareness. Its trunk — interacting with earth and sky —

represents mindfulness (*shema*): listening attentively as the Ground of our being nurtures us to listen attentively in the world of action.

Yet it is one tree: a union of attention and expression. Mozart could contemplate a complete symphony, then furiously pen the notes to manifest the masterpiece he had heard from start to finish in his head. Contemplation focuses the imagination to create keen action.

Life is ultimately defined by what we pay attention to. What we focus on feeds us — my translation of Ludwig Feuerbach's idea that "man is what he eats." Writing is a way of paying attention to things twice, savoring their layers, their essence. The same thing can be said of art, photography, cinema, music, dance, or any of the sciences. And each of these in turn depends on writing to pass on tools of the *trade*, as in the give and take that occurs in healthy commerce of life.

> Oh, Mama, just look at me one minute as though you really saw me.
>
> —Emily
> from Thornton Wilder's
> *Our Town*

Thomas Merton received countless letters demanding to know how he could produce so many books and pretend to keep a Trappist vow of silence in his hermitage at the Abbey at Gethsemani, Kentucky. He answered that writing was a form of contemplation, "writing and praying as I write." Since prayer is not the opposite of action, but rather a form of action, we could also say writing is a form of action. A group of Palestinian and Israeli authors gathered at the Sheikh Hussein Bridge, a symbolic link to Israel and Jordan, to discuss new ways to achieve peace in the Middle East. Israeli Etgar Keret described it as "kind of like an AA meeting. It's that kind of a support group" for writers on both sides to imagine a better future. The pen is mightier than the sword.

Most mornings, before beginning the day's work, I take some time to practice physical and spiritual exercises (like some in this book) and to write in my journal. But when I do serious writing, I hide away for a few days in a retreat center, a monastery, or our cottage in upstate New York. Since I frame writing as action, I tell myself to settle into contemplation first, so I can draw from its taproot while I write. A decade ago, at the Jesuit Spiritual Center in Wernersville, Pennsylvania, I wrote this prayer poem, and it now guides my writing for short or long periods.

WRITER'S ASCETICISM

Merton-like I hide away
to pray to write and pray
in this my hermitage,
to birth my heritage:
the gift of the burden,
the burden of the gift.

I invite you now to pause and reflect on the place writing has in your life: What gifts does writing bring? What struggles? What invitation do you sense in relation to your writing? (see exercise 2).

"Focal Experiences": Active Contemplation

Meaningful writing can spring from times of testing and gestating. John Fitzgerald Kennedy wrote his bestseller *Profiles in Courage* while flat on his bed from back surgery, on leave from the U.S. Senate. Laura

Hillenbrand wrote *Seabiscuit* from her bed of chronic pain that surely mirrors the broken horse and characters of the story. Life may hand us sabbath in the form of an illness, a car crash, a failed career. But how can we cultivate active contemplation without needing forced sabbaticals?

It begins with focusing on drops of experience all about us. High-tech environments insulate us from the throbbing messiness of nature, substituting the third-hand stress of cell phones, e-mail, and virtual conversations. After probing the impact of technology on culture for over two decades, philosopher Albert Borgmann coined the term "focal experiences."

> *You need to let the little things that would ordinarily bore you suddenly thrill you.*
>
> —Artist Andy Warhol
> *Love, Love, Love*

Direct and messy. Focal experiences refer to direct involvement in the blessed messiness of life. You change a diaper, get your nails dirty digging, smell a musty book, sit with a homeless person — or cook a meal from scratch. Focal experiences are about being present rather than alienated from life.

Take the example of food preparation. You can heat a frozen dinner in a microwave. By contrast, procuring the food, preparing it for guests, savoring the smells, serving the meal, lingering over conversation, and cleaning dishes becomes "a focal thing." And focal things ingrain us with focal practices, habits that promote mindfulness.

Often when I eat with a group I finish last, allowing time for more conversation. If someone notices my eating, I may say, "I'm on Thich Nhat Hanh's diet." What's that? Simple, fifty chews per bite! Well, maybe thirty. This Buddhist monk who witnessed daily violence to Vietnamese children caused by napalm and land mines, responded by founding the Buddhist School for Youth Social Service in Saigon. In his book *Anger*, Nhat Hanh says we overeat and gulp our food to numb ourselves. (In writing, gulping down huge slices of life dulls our keen observation of reality and takes away the raw tension.) The primal experience of eating is an excellent way to cultivate mindfulness in everything.

Here's how contemplative chewing works. First, by eating mindfully you slow down. Second, you savor each morsel. Third, you eat less because your stomach gets the message before that twenty-minute gap (when you normally keep eating) and says, "I'm satisfied!" Because of that you have more energy since your body becomes less tired and has less work to do. Fourth, there's more time for conversation, or if you're by yourself, for contemplation.

Eating and drinking can become practices to savor friendship, beauty, and life. "Most people drink coffee mindlessly from a cup held in one hand while doing some activity with the other," writes Paul Jones, former United Methodist pastor and now a Trappist monk. "In the monastery we have two-handled cups, for contemplative reasons . . . The monk grasps the fine shape of his cup with both hands and is thereby rendered unavailable to do anything except to be totally absorbed in the act of drinking, lost in the experience."

> *The world is charged with the grandeur of God . . . And for all this, nature is never spent; / There lives the dearest freshness deep down things.*
>
> —Gerard Manley Hopkins
> "God's Grandeur"

We cultivate focal practices by participating in play with our children, but not by parking them in front of a TV or feeding them a DVD or an iPOD. Even such tidy initials belie our compact shortcuts to living reality. Virtual chat rooms allow us to evade the give and take of real-time friendships. Of course, tech devices can also deepen lived experience, but that is the point: to be present to the raw stuff of life. So we can use arts and technology to re-present life, or to thirst for its deeper reality. That means showing up for life, self, and the Source of all life.

Another simple way to practice focal awareness is to carry a small magnifying glass. In *Lost in Wonder,* Esther de Waal tells how she will pull out her magnifying glass to look at a leaf, a twig, moss between concrete slabs, dandelions pushing up through gravel. What would lemon peels, paper, the texture of threads, or brush strokes in a Van Gogh print reveal?

Is this not close to what Jesus meant by considering the lilies of the field and the birds of the air? Is this not what Eastern traditions mean by mindfulness? I invite you in every occasion of happiness or danger to practice the response of guides like Moses, Isaiah, and Mary: "Here I am." The words can an act as a breath prayer for intense moments of crisis, or as a centering prayer for extended periods of meditation (see exercise 3).

By practicing focal awareness in simple matters we can train the soul to be *present*. Here I am, not there I might be. Here is why chemistry teachers still expose students to laboratory experiments where beakers break and smells may drive them from the room. Here is why some students of faith still learn original scriptural languages of Hebrew or Greek, Arabic or Aramaic, Sanskrit or Mandarin. Here is why people go on archeological digs or climb Everest. Here is why the disaster agency's budget manager needs to spend time with street level beneficiaries of the funds. Here and now experiences evoke something beneath facts. They take you across a primal threshold into spiritual insights nobody can teach you. One drop of experience may unlock a clue to the cosmos. It's like looking at the same facts and figures with a stereoscope.

Notice, notice, notice! And read, read, read! to harvest the observations of others. Then write, write, write! to get in touch with facts and feelings you didn't realize were there all along. Scientist Pierre Teilhard de Chardin wrote in *The Divine Milieu* that because of creation and, still more, of the Incarnation, nothing in our existence is ever mundane to those who know how to see. Your eye catches traces of grace in the grit.

Training the eyes of the heart to see links insight and action. Bobbie got involved in MADD (Mothers—*and others*—Against Drunk Driving, as she likes to say), after recovering from critical injuries in a car crash. One evening a state police officer presented the state MADD board with a group police photo for use in MADD advertising. Ordinarily a quiet person, Bobbie spoke out, "I don't see any women or people of color in this photograph." The police officials redid the photo. Sheer noticing became an act of justice.

"No thinking—that comes later. You must write your first draft with your heart. You rewrite with your head. The first key to writing is . . . to write, not to think!"

—Forrester in *Finding Forrester*

"Afternoon light marbling a white wall / Takes on the quality of revelation," writes May Sarton. Try a simple exercise of observation, by yourself or with a group. Have pen and paper handy. Focus on an object in the room where you are sitting. Allow a minute of silence. Then begin to write words or phrases *down* the page (see exercise 4).

The monk should be all eye.

—Abba Bessarion
fourth century

When the pupil is ready. Whatever your personal or professional pursuits, you can pause right now to ask, how can I create more focal engagement with things that concern me daily? For someone who thinks only about being homeless, every breath becomes a focal experience and every crumb of hope a focal thing. It's not that poverty is blessed, but a frozen rear or a scorched head makes one aware of every stitch of existence.

What do *you* wake up thinking about? Waking up means not taking it for granted. Maybe it's parenting. I watch a father talking on a cell phone while holding his son's hand as they walk through a park. I want to shout, "Wake up! Your son's going to die, and you too!" That father can be an economist and still enrich his trade by showing up with his son in the park.

Maybe it's science. Margaret J. Geller, senior scientist at the Smithsonian Astrophysics Observatory catches the value of such playful contemplation with a child, "Sometimes she'll be out digging in the dirt, and I think, I could try that!" And *that* is her next astronomical experiment.

Maybe it's philosophy or religion. You go to the library and find a rare book on Confucius. While there you strike up a conversation with a Hindu or an atheist. Both events become part of your research. Research means observing with the head *and* the heart, observing the data *and* the chance encounters in the process of discovering the data.

Now the Zen saying makes sense: "When the pupil is ready, the teacher will appear." If the pupil of your eye and your heart is wide awake, you can be digging or diapering or delving into books and your teachers appear out of nowhere. Sometimes the teacher *is* the garden or the child or the book, sometimes an insight from afar, sometimes the Hindu or the atheist who crosses your path.

But now try the saying in reverse: "When the teacher is ready, the pupil will appear." How can I explain the thread of providence that brought students and spiritual seekers to me when my life was ready? How can I explain how losing a cherished pulpit in a historic church morphed through a dark night into a new pulpit in the world through writing?

This is why a contemplative lens is not a luxury but a necessity for anyone who writes for love, labor, or learning. When the book is written in your heart, a publisher will appear. When the lesson is prepared in your mind, a classroom will appear. Later I'll talk about how to look for the classroom or the publisher in different guises—like the risen Christ showing up as a gardener or a fisher or a stranger. With this attitude, you can safely write your way home without worry of "success." Sometimes, though, you may want to prime the pump and carry a few buckets full of ideas and hopes back to the village to see if anyone is thirsty.

Connections, connections, connections. Only by drawing deeply from the well of contemplation can we really connect with the common stream of humanity's yearnings and learnings. Writing is all about making connections—with self, others, God and the universe of ideas, data, history, experiences, intuitions and hopes. In real estate, success is "location, location, location." But spiritually the strategy is connections, connections, connections.

In his bestseller *The Tipping Point,* Malcolm Gladwell shows how hard work alone is not the key to break-throughs in politics, ideas, show biz, or spirituality. It's the serendipity of con-nections and timing that can transform a chance encounter into a genuine rela-tionship or a cause worth dying for. Living with your pupils appropriately dilated is the key to catching sight of the miracle when the bush catches fire.

> Miracles seem to rest, not so much upon faces or voices or healing power coming suddenly near to us from far off, but upon our perceptions being made finer so that for a moment our eyes can see and our ears can hear that which is about us always.
>
> —Willa Cather
> *Death Comes for the Archbishop*

You can actually write your way into wonders you didn't know were there and surprise yourself at the end of the day. When you do that, the reader gets hooked, too. Robert Frost wrote, "No surprise in the writer, no surprise in the reader." As we will now explore, you can surprise yourself with facts—and feelings about the facts.

Critical and Creative Writing: Left Brain, Right Brain

The purpose of this little book is to show that contem-plation and action function as two seamless dimensions of a process that we can cultivate in both creative and critical writing. For a time I served as a hospital chaplain working with brain-injured and stroke patients and their families. That experience and my burgeoning shelf of books on the brain began to help me understand why we need community.

As a primarily right-brained individual I need to surround myself with people who are more left-brained to check the fine print. In her classic book *Drawing from the Right Side of the Brain,* Betty Edwards describes the basic inclination of left and right spheres. As a memory device, I think of the left hemisphere as more inclined to L words: linguistic, logical, linear and factual modes of thinking. I think of the right side as more inclined to R words: relational, rhythmic, aRtistic, cReative, and intuitive modes. The left is more analytical and time oriented, the right more integrative and space oriented.

Ideas *and* images. It's important to know that we all have a capacity for both critical (left hemisphere) expression and creative (right hemisphere) expression. A young adult once said to me, "I think I'm both right brained and left brained. I feel deeply about what I think about!" We'll come back to this in chapter 3 on methods (see exercises 16 and 17).

In *Writing with Power* Peter Elbow speaks of the seeming opposite skills of creativity and critical thinking working in tandem for both intuitive and consciously rational writing:

> The important thing is that you should exploit both intuition and conscious control, whichever kind of writing

you are doing. Conscious control needn't undermine the intuition you may use in writing poems and stories: you can conclude with critical thinking that the poem you wrote last night hangs together beautifully (perhaps even according to a principle you can't yet articulate) and by all means leave it alone. Similarly intuition needn't blunt your conscious awareness as you revise your essay today, just because last night you wrote seven nonstop pages that came from feelings and perceptions you didn't know you had. You can consciously and critically build your essay today out of insights you could only arrive at by relinquishing critical thinking last night.

I find the free flow of a blank journal serves as a laboratory to let the left-brain guards down as I write or draw or paint in a stream-of-consciousness style. For example, to reflect on a board meeting I may begin drawing stick figures around a table and end with a poem. However, many in younger generations have grown up naturally writing free flow and art with the computer. A lined pad can be a place to practice more informational writing: for example, how the global economy affects issues of spirituality and justice — or whether paying extra cash for fair trade coffee makes a difference. In any case, formal and informal writing need a vehicle to integrate reason and art, ideas and images (see resource 1).

Once while leading a workshop, the group began to compare writing with building a house with brick or stone — summarized in this prose poem.

YOUR WRITING HOUSE

If you are more left brained, cultivate free flow
writing. Stand back from your uniformly
shaped bricks and ask, what can make
the house more visually alive—arches, porches,
a bay window? If you are more right brained,
cultivate the art of sequencing, building your
house out of rough cut rocks—but create good,
solid mortar joints. Enhance the natural setting
of either house, incorporating touches
of beauty and subtle landscapes of rhyme,
humor, and stories.

Try out ways that combine both creative and critical
reflections. For example, you can write or type information your physician told you during your physical
exam, feelings it triggered in you, and some exercises
you want to engage in to keep your body, heart, mind,
and spirit healthy.

Once when I did this I realized I didn't know the
medical names and locations of many body parts. It
sent me scurrying to a medical guide, and I doodled a
sketch of my body in my journal. Labeling major
parts with medical names gave me a new appreciation
for my body's complex simplicity. So you might
prayerfully sketch your body, noting areas you've
learned that need attention. Try writing a prayer
poem that gathers up fears and hopes about your
health. Finally, practice a focal experience as you
gratefully notice each part of your body, one breath
at a time, focusing first on the soles of your feet and
ending with the top of your head. The writing has

permeated your body. Pause now. Treat yourself to this experience (see exercise 5).

Fragments from my journal can make their way into my formal writing. I often use the journal to write about blocks in my writing; some of these scribblings morph into prayer poems that you can read in this book. Or I'll explore a wild idea I'm not ready to put in print. Occasionally I dig into past journals and unearth deeper layers of meaning and shards from past feasts; experience reflected upon yields new treasures for the journey.

> *Nobody sees a flower— really—it is so small—we haven't time, and to see takes time, like to have a friend takes time.*
>
> —Georgia O'Keeffe
> American Commemoratives,
> 1996

Repositioning the Easel: Observing from a Different Angle

Toward the end of my sabbatical in India, I remembered suggestions from a friend about visiting the Taj Mahal. The result created multiple experiences of that one incredible world wonder. My wife had joined me when we arrived on a sweltering afternoon amid myriad faces and languages and light so bright we could hardly see the building directly. Then we remembered to step back beneath a cloistered porch to see the noble treasure silhouetted in an archway of time. Up close, we saw its mammoth but disfigured granite blocks, then felt dizzy as we tilted our heads skyward.

That is when I recalled my friend's well-kept secret: for a few extra rupees we could take a rowboat across a small river to the backside. Standing quietly on the far bank with only a few Indian people and viewing its simple stately beauty minus a few front-side adornments, the river offered us an amazing gift: the mirror image of the Taj Mahal, shimmering, majestic.

The ultimate vista awaited us as we returned at sunrise to an un-peopled pristine view of the massive white jewel, flanked by luminous garden pools. As an anticlimax, from the porch of a mile-away prison, we took away the same bird's-eye view as its builder Emperor Shah Jahan. There, imprisoned by his son, the emperor died grieving his favorite wife buried in the Taj Mahal.

When you contemplate things from different angles, your mental frame of reference changes. And when you write out of the stream of your reflections at varied points of time and place, your emotional frame of reference changes. You may even see facts and facets that were completely hidden before you pondered and penned your way into it from a new angle.

Contemplate some persistent family- or work-related issue. Then write into it from a different year, season, century, context, culture, age (as a child or an adult), or voice (in the third person, as if observing yourself). Or try it the other way around: first write from the different perspective. Then afterward ponder how you've surprised yourself. Or let it all happen at once: spend time in quiet pondering before writing, ponder through your fingertips as you write, and when you're done, push the chair back and ponder what happened.

Write about a problem from the future, like George Orwell's *1984*. Or from a make-believe place, like Tolkien's Middle-Earth. Worriers have active imaginations. So use your creative gift to create optional endings to the same predicament. That's the stuff novels are made of. That's why they're called novels—they give you a novel slant on the peculiar dynamics of life.

The way you design your writing and meditating environment can set the mood for a different place or time and cultivate focal awareness. In my writing den, I can pause to ring a Tibetan singing bowl, gaze at an icon of Luke writing his Gospel, or glance at Van Gogh's *Starry Night*. I sense generations buoying me up as I write, subliminally aware of classic quotes, nature photos, and postcards from friends around the world—all tacked to a cork wall—and books on books in the adjoining room. The French artist Claude Monet would paint the same cathedrals and bridges in differ-ent hours of the day, seasons, lighting, or weather, thus creating ever new experiences for the viewer. The tides of perspective carry you far and near, high and low.

What happens when you reposition the easel? Does the subject itself change? Or do you? Or like a Möbius strip, is it really all a single edge rippling around showing itself to you as if again for the first time?

Here's an idea for speaking or teaching. A minister told how he preached on the overly familiar parable of the Prodigal Son from the neighbor's point of view, in first person: Let me tell you about this dysfunctional family that lived next door. That kid was spoiled rotten. He insulted his dad, but guess what that father did? Yep. Let his son run off with the family money. And that mother—ever notice she's invisible in that story?—that's because she never left the house after that. Just grieved inside. Older brother worked 24/7 but felt no thanks from Pop. Now, what do you think happened when that wasted brother came home? Did he get a beating? No, his pop threw him a party. And you should have watched that well-behaved older brother blow up!

By shifting the easel to the neighbor's voice, the speaker reconstructed the original tension in the story: the father (God?) now seems as dysfunctional as the rest of the family (see exercise 6).

Moving the easel into strange places. Robert Hunter's lyrics invite us to look in strange places to see the light. Sometimes I'm the one who needs to pick up my easel and go to a far country in order to come to myself, arise and return home as if for the first time. To do this requires courage, to leave the comfort zone of my own familiarity. Annie Dillard advises young writers, "If you have a choice, live at least a year in very different parts of the country."

In most of my travels abroad and even in the United States, I keep my ears and eyes open for connections with grassroots people in an area that draws me. The connections often happen by surprise, through friends or friends of friends in places I travel, at churches, concerts, ballparks, or professional gatherings far and near.

In the space of one week the same person asked me three times to let him know if I was going back to India. The third time I surprised myself by proclaiming, "If I go anywhere next it's going to be Latin America." Amazingly, the next week I received an e-mail from a former student's wife in Guatemala—copied to several

Once in a while you get shown the light / in the strangest of places if you look at it right.

—Robert Hunter
"Scarlet Begonias"

potential retreat leaders. Would one of us consider coming to lead their annual retreat?

In a matter of months I found myself in another strange country, but always at home and gifted by newfound teachers. "Travel is fatal to prejudice," wrote Mark Twain. Putting yourself in someone else's turf shakes you loose from your own ingrained habits.

Spiritual chiaroscuro. Photographers know about being shown the light in strange places. Their skill comes in looking at it right. Dorothea Lange and Walker Evans began taking pictures of forgotten people early in the last century, and they became pioneers of the photo essay as a whole new form of communication. They introduced poor people's faces into millions of American homes in newspapers and magazines long before TV and the Internet.

I refer to this analogy of lighting in writing as "spiritual chiaroscuro" or "literary chiaroscuro." Picture a Rembrandt painting. The highlighted subjects leap out at you, silhouetted by the backdrop of massive darks and shadows. The same is true of a black and white photo by Civil War photographer Mathew Brady. T. S. Eliot described it with the metaphor "light dappled with shadows."

Translate this into life. If you want to find new light, then enter into the dark places in the same old stuff you deal with every day, or in the stuff you keep avoiding. There you will find diamonds ready for the cutting. The Hebrew prophet Isaiah described it in chapter 45: "I will give you treasures of darkness and riches hidden in secret places."

Nobody wants advice. If you want to pass on your cherished values and your deepest vulnerabilities, find a way to tell the stories of your struggles and faith. Or give someone a discerning question to ponder. Let people hear compassion in your tone of voice, see it in your countenance, and sense it between the lines of your letters and e-mails. "Tell all the Truth, but tell it slant": Emily Dickinson understands the subtle power of indirection through hints in stories, parables, or poetic images. Pure light will blind a person. Light dappled with real shadows can be carried in the heart.

Another way to angle the easel is to read your writing aloud to yourself, to a trusted friend, or to a group. Or ask someone else to read it to you. But maybe you can't write your way home until you tell your way home first. If so, find the friend or a group and tell the story. Maybe you can write it after you experience hearing your own words.

For a few people, writing with your own hand may not be the way. Oral tradition has nurtured humanity's life on the planet through myriad primal epochs, contrasted to the brief slice of human written traditions. As in Celtic and many native cultures, you may be privileged to record your ancestors' vanishing stories, so they won't be lost forever. Or ask someone to record your stories if you have the courage to disclose them with trusted friends. However it works, I pray your stories and questions find their way onto the pages of peoples' hearts.

The more we get in touch with our own inner scripts, the more we get in touch with the ocean of treasures in the world around us. Cellist Yo-Yo Ma is recognized not only for the excellence of his music but also for building musical bridges around the globe. When asked what sends him out there to play with Appalachian fiddlers or drummers from India or indigenous artists of Mongolia or Azerbaijan, he answers that so much of human expression is longing. The longing draws us toward some vision as parents, as human beings, as citizens.

That longing ignites spiritual questions every good writer and reader of life needs to ask: "Where is our country headed? Where am I in this global village? What part can I play in what it can become?"

Ma wants his music to evoke the wandering and wondering. I am reminded of two keys to Jesus' teaching—penetrating stories and provocative questions: "What do you think? A man had two sons . . ." Stories of human impasses create paradoxes and get people buzzing about the way things are and what they might become. Wandering brings you face to face with wonder. You can start with sandcastles (see exercise 7).

Monday Evening

After napping under Gram's beach umbrella late Monday afternoon, Marin loses herself in building sandcastles. She cries a bit when a huge wave demolishes the first one. But she just builds another and another, inching closer to the beach as the water advances. She feels no pressure, only pleasure. Right before leaving the beach, she asks Gram to take a photo of her sitting next to her fanciest architectural wonder, complete with moat, tunnel, and turrets. Years later, after she's gone miles offshore, she'll return to sandcastle dreams at a new level.

By bedtime this girl's head is buzzing with all the things she's observed. Her wanderings have only piqued her wonder. "Why are the waves so foamy? How come the water's icy cold? Why was the sun so big and red tonight?"

Holding a conch shell to her ear with one hand she says, "Shhhh! Listen to the ocean!" In the other hand she clasps an elliptical bit of driftwood with a knot for an eye and says, "Look at my fish!" Gram smiles. Drifting into wonderland, Marin dreams of going out into the crashing waves tomorrow —from safe observation to scary wading.

EXERCISE 2   *Reviewing Your Writing: Gifts? Obstacles? Invitation?*

I invite you now to pause and scan over the ways writing happens in your life, and focus on a recent period of time— say the past week or month. Now ponder **gifts** you experience through your writing . . . **struggles** or **obstacles** you encounter in writing . . . and some **invitation** you sense in relation to your writing. What's the lure, the draw? See if a word or phrase, or an image or metaphor comes to mind that gathers up your hope regarding writing as you begin this book. Now take your journal and record these three areas above. Find a way to converse with someone.

"Here I Am": Centering Word or Phrase

Quietly slow down your breathing, with a prayer to be present. Gently begin to say within yourself, "Here I am" (*hineni* in Hebrew)—the human response of Moses, Abraham, Isaiah, and of Mary to divine Presence. Spend a few minutes simply repeating the phrase in rhythm to your breathing: "Here I am . . . " (or *hineni* . . .) or just "Here . . . " Imagine yourself being present to your self . . . to your surroundings . . . to the Spirit . . . the Spirit being present to you. Let go of the phrase, or return to it if distracted. (You might begin with five minutes, then try working up to fifteen or twenty. It can be freeing to set a handheld alarm or a kitchen timer.) Reflect, using your journal.

Meditating on an Object in the Room

Have your pen handy and open to a clean page in your journal (or on your computer). Probably the biggest barrier to journaling or writing for others is being too self-critical, writing out of the head instead of the heart. To break through the impasse, I suggest a simple method. Set a timer for about five minutes. Keep your hands open, not yet writing. Now let your eye fall on an object in the room where you're sitting. Contemplate it for one minute. Then begin to write words or phrases *down* the page (instead of complete sentences from left to right). Stop in five minutes—and place an ellipsis at the end . . . (indicating there may be more). Read over it in silence. If possible, now find someone to listen as you read it aloud (in person or by phone). Ask the person to be attentive to your tone of voice, your countenance—and notice any "shift" from the outward object to something deeper. (If you're face-to-face, reciprocate with the other person.)

Meditative Thanks with Your Body

Sit in stillness, and slow down your breathing. Allow a centering word or phrase to arise (like "Here I am," exercise 3), or a quieting image, such as a babbling brook. Repeat it slowly, using the word or image. In many spiritual traditions, the body is the temple of the Spirit. In Christian tradition, worship begins by presenting one's body. Inhale lovingly . . . meditate . . . exhale thankfully . . . Begin inhaling while tensing your left foot, then release it when exhaling . . . right foot . . . left ankle . . . etc., each area of the body up through your abdomen . . . to your heart . . . then each shoulder, arm, hand . . . return to your larynx . . . parts of the face . . . to the top of your head. Gratefully bask in an aura of peace. When you finish the exercise, you may take your journal and write a few reflections from the experience.

Option: In your journal, doodle a pencil sketch of your body; note areas that need attention.

Contemplating and Writing from a Different Angle

Open to a clean page in your journal or computer. Quietly ponder before writing, ponder through your fingertips as you write, and ponder when you finish. First, sit down now and take a few moments to scan over your life, noticing some family, relational, or work-related concern. Prayerfully observe your feelings, visualizing faces of persons involved and physical surroundings. Next, contemplate without thinking: take a few deep breaths, relinquishing the issue with each breath, perhaps by repeating a centering word or phrase—or an image. After a few minutes, write into the issue from a different year, season, century, context, culture, age (as a child or an adult), or voice (in the third person, as if observing yourself), or from the future. You might create optional endings to the problem. Finally, push your chair back or sit back and ponder what you have written and how you are feeling. Then read it aloud—or ask someone to read it to you.

Writing about Sandcastles

Prepare for deepening your writing life by imagining the beach, observing sights, sounds, smells, and other people. Then imagine building a sandcastle, letting it take shape in your mind's eye. Take a mental photo of it, and watch it as a wave smashes it to nothing. When you have finished the visualization, begin to write word pictures in prose or poetic style. When you have finished, read it aloud to someone else. Then ask that person to read it aloud to you.

Ongoing practice: You can engage in "sandcastle writing" on any subject without pressure to produce or keep anything. Experienced writers who've gone far out will return to the shoreline to build sandcastle dreams, toying with ideas and fantasies that leave no mark except in the playroom of your experience.

Wading—Focus on Wonder

Childlike playfulness coupled with complex ideas

Tuesday Morning

Marin's second day at the beach shifts from observing at a distance to wading right into the wonder of the waves. This morning she meets another seven-year-old in the next-door condo whose idea of water is "no fear." Aguar lived in a house off the Philippine coast, diving by age four when he came to the United States with his dad (Miguel) and Lolo (grandpa) Ibarra. Everyone is delighted, especially Gram and Lolo. Now the grandparents can take turns watching the two kids play while Miguel goes away for a week on his cruise-ship job.

But Monday's child still feels a bit self-conscious, looking around to see if Gram thinks she's exploring too far with her new friend. Lolo calls them back to look through his telephoto lens to observe light glistening on the waves. They're impatient with secondhand wonder; the ocean wins.

Kicking off his flip-flops, Aguar grabs a beach ball and dashes into the freezing shoal, skipping through pebbles to land in the nearest wave. He throws the ball in mid-air— the ideal lure for Marin to run splashing into the crest. Monday is spent observing from outside, Tuesday from inside. Wading is observation with skin on.

Sometimes you take a long, slow look at a thing for years before ever venturing into the wonder of it. Other times you get caught up in a moment of pristine, spine-tingling wonder, and only later stand back to reflect on it. Here we have two sides of the same experience, like the Tao of the yin and yang symbol. Writing provides the skin for both kinds of observation. But it usually starts bit by bit.

Wade in the Water

It's a dangerous thing to start wading if you haven't spent time observing where the rocks are, the way the sand shifts, and how to back off if the waves crest too high. You may head off in the wrong direction and get swallowed up in such a whale of wonder, like Jonah, that it turns sour and spits you out.

Wading can be treacherous without learning to swim or dive—or surf. To wade out even a few inches means stepping foot into the deep Mystery of life and love and its mighty forces of danger and delight.

Once you start wading into the wonder you're hooked. Frederick Douglass, a child slave who would become a brilliant writer, educator, and orator, overheard his master say it was a dangerous thing for a slave to learn to read and write. "From that moment, I understood the pathway from slavery to freedom," wrote Douglass. He had mastered four letters and boasted that he could draw them better than white boys. Daring them to write better, he tricked the other letters and words from them one by one. He had gained the treasured ship that would transport his ideas into writings and lectures amid the fierce tides of resistance and freedom.

Wade in the water, wade in the water children,
Wade in the water, God's gonna trouble the water.

In code language this African American spiritual song encrypts *wade* and *trouble* with profound double meanings. "Wade in the water" signifies the political clue of crossing a river (the Bible's Red Sea) out of slavery in the American South (Egypt). It also signifies the spiritual clue of the paralyzed man who tells Jesus he has no one to put him in the pool when the water is "troubled"—the time of healing.

Paradoxically a troubling situation begets healing and purpose. The song cryptically proclaims a radical spiritual release in baptism and at the same time bathes the imagination with hope for political release (via the Underground Railroad). Contemplation of "safe" biblical images serves as a springboard to countercultural action.

In a primarily oral culture, music provides the text and texture for words to infiltrate the soul (body, mind, and spirit) with a child-like yet radical lullaby of singing and swaying, drumming and dancing. Writing that's good for the soul, no matter what the subject, is born out of such primal experiences that tap into the child in each of us.

The "Child" in Spiritual Traditions

No child who observes water for long can resist the lure to wade into it. In religious traditions, to advance spiritually means returning to a childlike habit of mind. The great person is one who does not lose the child's heart: so Confucian leader Mencius expressed it in the third century BCE. When disciples ask Jesus who is the greatest in the kingdom, he sets a child among them and says, "Truly I tell you, unless you change and become like children, you will never enter the kingdom of heaven"(Matthew 18:3). The Sufi poet Hafiz asks God to "take care of that / Holy infant my heart has become."

CHILDREN

We are children first,
   then try feverishly
   to become adults,
   until painfully
we become children again.
   And again . . .

Sadly, between birth and adulthood much of the spontaneity of dancing, drumming, drawing, and dreaming gets squeezed out of us. Every human being is born out of the waters of the womb. That is why in dreams and mythology water often represents that pre-conscious self with unconscious connections to the mythical and spiritual truths of ancient generations. As we shall see, scientific discoveries often have amazing connections to mythical stories or dream symbols. Wading into the unconscious initiates us with fresh splashes of surprise.

Like dreams, fairy tales are full of two forms of sur-prise—as in serendipity and wonder, and as in shock and trauma. Bruno Bettelheim's observation in *The Uses of Enchantment* strikes a universal chord: the fairy tale will continue to speak in every age of life because it gives voice to the monsters and fantasies in all of us.

When you wade into the bubble or the rubble of surprise you are connecting with the spiritual dimension of the child. I invite you now to pause before reading on, and to contemplate the qualities of a child, journaling in your mind or on paper (see exercise 8).

As I write, devastating war reports threaten to kidnap my spirit and make what I'm doing seem insignificant in the face of world violence. Then I tell myself if I get sucked into this hole of futility, I'll do nothing to bring peace. In one such time I let myself play around with the image of my pen as a sword.

> *I want to write, but more than that, I want to bring out all kinds of things that lie buried in my heart.*
>
> —Anne Frank
> *The Diary of a Young Girl*

WHOLLY DISTURBANCE

War news takes over.
Let this disturbance
become the troubled
waters into which I delve
my pen to write my way
down and back again,
coaxing others to selve
into their own
turbulent healing.
   This pen is mightier
   than that sword.

In *Growing Young*, the late Princeton anthropologist Ashley Montagu advocates for a lifelong process of "neoteny," cultivating the qualities of a child: "The need to love others and to be loved; the qualities of curiosity, inquisitiveness, open-mindedness, experimental-mindedness; the sense of humor, playfulness, joy, the optimism, honesty, resilience, and compassionate intelligence — that constitute the spirit of the child."

YOUTHING

Hold onto love,
let go of youth.
Be held by love:
Behold the child
in you come forth!

Writing begins by wading into the script that lies buried in the ocean of the heart. Physically, wading takes place where an expanse of land meets an expanse of water — so in our doodling and dawdling we begin to explore the shoreline between conscious and unconscious life. Again, it is no coincidence that so many spiritual encounters take place by the shore. The shoreline signifies the liminal space where REM sleep occurs, or where in a moment of not thinking about a problem, insight dawns. The shoreline is the place where playing can become the most serious praying.

The script that lies buried in the heart may differ wildly from person to person — drama for Shakespeare, sonatas for Mozart, a starry night for Van Gogh, science for Galileo, soul-force (*satyagraha*) for Gandhi and King, dignity for Rosa Parks, poetry for Maya Angelou.

Contemplative play in art, politics, and science.
Creative breakthroughs wed the most advanced theories
of science or politics or meaning with
the innocent wonder of a child. Howard
Gardner shows how childlike qualities
motivated artists like Pablo Picasso and
choreographers like Martha Graham
and scientists like Einstein; they also
underlie the political innovation of
Gandhi. "Do not despise my opinion
when I remind you that it should not
be hard for you to stop sometimes and
look into the stains of walls, or ashes or a fire, or clouds
or mud or like places, in which, if you consider them
well, you may find really marvelous ideas," Leonardo da
Vinci advised readers of his notebooks. "By indistinct
things the mind is stimulated to new inventions."

> *The best scientists are those who retain the somewhat naïve curiosity of a child. They see the world with a special eye.*
>
> —Margaret Geller, chief scientist at the Smithsonian Astrological Observatory

Though contemplation in spiritual traditions conveys a specialized meaning of a deep form of wordless
prayer, to contemplate even the surface stuff of ordinary reality can open the door to the deeper Reality.
There is really only one Reality, as with the cyclical
image of the Möbius strip. William Blake bids us "to
see the World in a Grain of Sand." Contemplation by
simple mindfulness in everyday things is like the first
ring in the onion leading to contemplation of the Holy
at the center of all things. So Leonardo can recom-
mend contemplating stains on walls, mud, fire, ashes,
or clouds. Such things sound a lot like kindergarten or
nursery school (see exercise 9).

We are programmed to consider such mindless gazing into space as a waste. Yet scientists like artists

know that what is most real often rises out of empty space. Writing into the shoals of the unconscious can edge us into the truth that permeates all existence. Many of the best insights come unbidden in a moment of *not* thinking directly about the subject.

Prayer means turning to Reality.

—Evelyn Underhill
The Spiritual Life

Haydn and Mozart made use of unconscious urges or sleep states; Wagner composed parts of *Die Meistersinger* in a dream-like condition.

After working in the chemistry lab to discover the molecular structure of benzene, a young professor came home for supper. Dozing afterward near a fireplace in 1859, Friedrich August Kekulé von Stradoinitz dreamed of the ancient symbol of a serpent biting its tail. Kekulé feverishly gathered data validating his intuition—still known as the theory of the Benzene ring.

While boarding a streetcar in Zurich, a self-taught student glanced at the town clock and instantly "knew" E=MC². The "acorn" of Albert Einstein's whole career in miniature cracked open: from a kid who did poorly in school to the most brilliant human being of his time.

"Wait, I think we have touched something very important here. Let's not talk about it . . . Let's wait for two weeks, and let it solve itself." So Werner Heisenberg, Nobel Prize winner, famous for the uncertainty principle of quantum physics, would speak to his researcher in the middle of some problem.

Wading sounds like waiting, and either can feel so unproductive compared to making a presentation or completing a project. Sabbath practices such as periods for silence and meditation leave no visible evidence. Your head keeps giving marching orders, "Do something useful!"

A day or two into one of my writing retreats I call home and hear, "How's it going?" I say, "I'm just wading, going over the same old ground." Later, I do start swimming and diving into it, eventually floating—where the writing carries me. But then I get back home and lose the flow. It's just wading again for weeks. That's why I tell writers' groups, "Wade a little bit every day." You might even tap or type into bits of wonder.

Wading is basically playing—tinkering, toying, fooling around. It lacks the intensity of swimming, our next chapter's theme on serious methods to integrate writing with contemplation. Yet sometimes we have to discipline ourselves to return to playing and get captured again by wonder. Without the wonder, the best methods for writing and life become a drag.

> *In short, you can enhance your creativity by playfully altering your perceptions and trying to look beyond the obvious, most practical interpretations of what you see around you.*
>
> —Richard Restak
> *Mozart's Brain and the Fighter Pilot*

Multiple Intelligences: Communicating with Soul

To restore the healthy child in us is to live with soul. You can find scores of books with soul in the title: *Soul Mates, The Soul of Soil, The Soul of a New Machine, Care of the Soul, Seat of the Soul, The Soul of Leadership,* and *Chicken Soup for the Soul* in all its sequels. Why are folks lured to *soul*?

In Jewish tradition soul (*nefesh*) embodies the whole person: "Bless the LORD, O my soul, and all that is

within me, bless [God's] holy name" (Psalm 103:1).
The *Shema,* the most important daily prayer that Jesus
quoted many times, bids you to *listen* and "love the
LORD your God with all your heart, with all your soul
and with all your might" (Deuteronomy 6:4;
Mark 12:29).

Educator Howard Gardner's Multiple Intelligences
approach to learning offers frames for integrating all
of life. Some intelligences are highly developed in a
person, others less, yet everyone has some aptitude
in each.

To restore the soul is to renew the healthy child in
us, awake with all the senses. But *soul* sounds diffuse,
nonquantifiable. What practical ways can we restore
soul to our working, parenting, recreating, and communicating? We cannot *do* the restoring; we can only
train the eye of awareness, the fingers of expression,
and the figures of speech. Here I offer a brief playful
perspective. (For a more complete application, see
resource 2, Multiple Intelligences.)

1. *Linguistic/verbal:* Play with words, sounds, and
   signs.
2. *Logical/mathematical:* Play with numbers and
   puzzlers; toy with ideas.
3. *Spatial/visual:* Play with images, shapes, space,
   and imagination.
4. *Musical/rhythmic:* Play with drums, strings, tones,
   rhymes, and puns.
5. *Kinesthetic/bodily:* Play physically—dance, sports,
   gestures, drama, and mime.
6. *Interpersonal:* Play with others—games, jokes,
   tricks, humor, and songs.

7. *Intrapersonal:* Play with your inner child: dreams, musings, insights, and Ahas!

8. *Naturalist:* Play with birds, trees, water, stars, wonder, and cycles of birth-decay.

9. *Existentialist:* Play with "why" questions like a two-year-old.

Creative story draws on all nine modes: witness stories as operas, musicals, ballads, dances, and dramas. Stories are relational and linear; they paint pictures and embody gestures, create space and connections (right brain); they contain facts and ideas and create a story line (left brain). Stories connect all ages and all levels of education.

Communicating with soul restores childlike qualities that integrate body, mind, and spirit so all of life morphs into a playful, prayerful classroom. Emotional and spiritual intelligences weave through all nine: Archimedes ran naked out of his bath when a new scientific truth struck him, shouting, *Eureka! Eureka!*—"I've found it!" Pascal encountered the mystic Christ via mathematical calculations.

In contemplating and communicating life we can use language to embody ideas, pictures, gestures, rhythm, silence, relationships, nature, and questions. I will weave these nine modes throughout coming chapters.

> Only when I make room for the child's voice within me do I feel genuine and creative.
>
> —Alice Miller
> writing on childhood trauma
> and creativity

Playing with words. A thousand times when I'm fussed I tell myself to return to childlike wonder. Yet I ask myself, how? While I was in India for a thirty-day retreat to pray with Ignatius of Loyola's Spiritual Exercises, poetry started coming. I couldn't sleep with the noise of barking dogs at night, chanting from mosques in wee hours, planes and trains by day. I got annoyed. Everything I knew about retreat was to rest, but I couldn't.

An avalanche of poems cascaded in my head. What to do? *Just be still,* I told myself. I would crawl out of bed through my mosquito net in the dark (there was no electricity during the night) and scribble the poem—maybe then I'd be rid of it so I could sleep. Then another would occur, like this one:

INDIA VIGILS

At 4 a.m.
I am not sure
if the blare I hear
is the sound of a mosque
or a fierce mosquito
near my ear.
But I am sure
it is a call to prayer.

That morning I met with my Jesuit spiritual director, Charles, and I complained about the noise. He showed me an exercise from his late Jesuit friend and guru Anthony de Mello, to train myself to listen for the silence beyond the noise. By putting my thumbs in my ears for a few minutes, then releasing them, I could listen through the noise into the silence beyond the sounds. The noise had taught me a new contemplative skill (see exercise 10).

I complained how the poems kept my mind abuzz, when I knew that spiritual retreat *should* be about emptying the mind. My guide reminded me of de Mello's phrase that he had shared with me while standing beneath the moonlight: "Let the child in you come forth."

We concluded that one of the ways I play is to play with words. Since Ignatius encourages the retreatant to use his or her imagination while praying with scriptures, here I was playing *and* praying at the same time — while using scriptures! (My poem "India Vigils" had tweaked the theme of "staying awake" from Matthew 26:40-46.) I mentioned a rabbinic saying that the Sabbath is to play and to pray. With that my guide got up and placed his old 1950s manual typewriter in my hands, blessing my word playing as prayer.

One February I went to our cottage "to pray to write and pray" — because I know in my head that my best writing comes out of stillness. But I was too wired to take time for contemplation; I wanted to dive right in and write. So I physically put myself in a different space. I had the key to a little Episcopal chapel and let myself into the freezing building, and sat there on my hands — partly to warm myself but mainly to keep myself from writing. After half an hour or so, two people walked in to view the stained glass windows. I was hardly aware as they came and left. By then I had no trouble walking around gazing at the frozen lake and sitting on a rock in the sun. At dusk the writing gushed forth and I lost track of time.

I have returned to this practice many times since to coach myself into a playful, prayerful place, and invite others to try it. I sometimes say I have "theological ADHD"—a short attention span with God.

But all this is for the sake of the central question: how do you cultivate childlike wonder? As another simple method, you can prompt playful imagination in writing everyday memos and notes at home or work (see exercise 11).

Playful projects for serious purposes. A series of devastating earthquakes had been in the news. I was fascinated to hear a report on how rescue dogs are trained to go into rubble to sniff out humans. It all begins as play, like hide and seek. Dogs are enticed to go behind certain trees: find a humanoid, get a reward—no humanoid, no reward. I recalled a third-hand phrase I heard somewhere: "playful projects for serious purposes."

Knowledge is limited. Imagination encircles the world.

—Albert Einstein
in *Saturday Evening Post,* 1929

Once while I was telling this story, a woman who is blind spoke up. Her dog, Jazz, had been commissioned to the Ground Zero rescue in New York City in 2001. "Things got so awful," she said, "the dogs got so discouraged that play sessions had to be scheduled with live persons to renew the dogs' spirits."

The Buddha laughs. Zorba dances. Jesus has fun while doing good—often on the Sabbath—partying, and playing with words as he tells about a party, or gets himself invited to another. Yet it is all for the most serious purpose: the soul's connection with its own Ground. Rooted in the Ground of all Being, like the giant sequoias, the soul grows strong by connecting its roots with nature, neighbors, and nations.

Playing with tensions. Play does not arrive without tension, all warm and fuzzy, by avoiding the cold prickly currents. Rather a playful, resilient spirit emerges by wading into the grit of fear and grief. The Russian writer Maxim Gorky could talk of playing with sorrow like a child's toy and making a carnival of grief.

But why words? Why not an unmediated experience of "carnival"? Words act as miniature vehicles to make the carnival present. Words become ponies on a merry-go-round, curves on a roller coaster, music from a calliope—carrying you through, above, and beneath the grief. True, the transformation of grief also takes place via canvas and clay, drums and drama, but words provide the subterranean vehicles for any artist's imagination. Why words? Emily Dickinson writes: "A word is dead / When it is said, / Some say. / I say it just / Begins to live / That day."

Wading into Resistance with Humor, Stories, and Questions

Writing without resistance is boring. The paradoxical connection of playfulness and seriousness begets a healthy tension. Wading moves beyond flat observation, taking the first steps into experiencing the currents of resistance. It's the difference between a predictable indoor pool and the lure of the ocean with its ebb and tide.

> *If you can't swim, wade.*
> —Cynthia Copeland Lewis
> *Really Important Stuff My Kids
> Have Taught Me*

How can you get the currents going in your indoor pool if you're nowhere near the ocean? Practice doing laps by forcing yourself to write nonstop for ten minutes, raising questions and answering back. In a word, add *resistance*.

Address serious issues "from the backside." Suppose you're preparing a major presentation of the tree commission to the township board. Pause to contemplate. Imagine individuals who think of trees as mere obstacles in the way of shopping malls. Frame questions and arguments they would pose. Meditate to recall stories of real-life examples.

The same method works for writing essays, sermons, teaching notes, devotional readings—or your required report in the organization's newsletter. Dramatize an issue with some tension and catch the reader's attention. Then zoom in with your creative idea.

It also works wonders in personal journaling. After my father died, by having a dialogue with him about his verbal nonresponsiveness, I began understanding him and that nonresponsive part of myself. Then I discovered he expressed himself through intuition and gestures, and I could celebrate these gifts in myself.

By creating an antagonist's voice in your writing, you've unearthed a hidden edge of your own of misgivings—and those of your reader. C. S. Lewis does this masterfully in *The Screwtape Letters*, where the chief devil Screwtape trains his nephew apprentice Wormwood. Lewis upends things as Screwtape refers to God as "the Enemy" and the believer as "the patient." The result is hilarious!

Practice by setting up playful tension in casual encounters. While I was walking my dog one day, a five-year-old boy asked me how old our little Sheltie was. I answered, "One hundred five!" That, of course, led to a conversation about one dog year being about like seven human years.

Recording minutes of committee meetings usually ranks second on the boredom scale only compared to the affliction of reading them. Not so with Anne's. Her first set of minutes was spiced with humor. "Just before the dinner break, Mary left the meeting to assume the role of Martha in the kitchen." No one dared ask for a "straight" set for the official record. Another time Anne wrote, "Kim moved that board members voluntarily fast for one meal during its annual retreat. At this point, Nate's stomach growled to second the motion." Everyone read those minutes.

Convert Insights into Questions and Stories

Have fun with tension by converting your insights into questions and stories, like Socrates and Zen masters, Sufi mystics, and rabbis—including Jesus. A scribe asks, "What do I do to inherit eternal life?" Jesus volleys back, "How do you read the law?" When Jesus applauds the scribe's answer—love God and your neighbor—the scribe retorts: "But who is my neighbor?" Jesus volleys again with the story of the "Good Samaritan," a moral outcast who rescues a good guy beaten by robbers (Luke 10:29-37). Jesus serves one final time with another question: "Which one proved neighbor to the man who fell among the robbers?" The insight has been implanted via interactive questions and stories.

Deepen suspense by telling stories that evoke questions and more stories. Watch how Aunt Essie's tales trigger others at the family picnic. Scholars, too, often weave their research by building up to obstacles and surprise incidents that grab your attention.

In his bestseller *A Short History of Almost Everything,* Bill Bryson describes graduate student Clair Patterson's elation the day he calculated the age of the earth. He was so ecstatic he drove from Chicago to his boyhood town in Iowa and checked himself into a hospital, afraid he had a heart attack. Yet Patterson spent the rest of his life battling corporations successfully to get lead out of our gasoline and homes, with no public honors. You don't have to be Bill Bryson to discover an unsung hero. Pause now, and see if you can recall an experience where a gift emerged through a time of struggle with or without recognition (see exercise 12).

Questions and stories get people searching their souls, probing beneath accepted platitudes. What gets unearthed—even if it appears totally "secular"—is a layer of prayer, a yearning for something deeper. As with an archeological dig, one chance opening can unearth an artifact of grace. That one artifact may lead to the treasure that signals your life's direction or upends your universe.

There are years of our lives that ask questions and years that answer.

—Zora Neale Hurston
Their Eyes Were Watching God

An ordinary book review can set up this holy tension. Traditionally, reviewers analyze a book's content "objectively" and list a few shortcomings and reasons I should buy or not buy the tome. But not the one I read this morning. In *The Christian Century's* review of William Zinsser's newest book, Betty Smart Carter begins by telling about a series of emotional crises in her own life. Afterward, she "felt the great bird of autobiography roosting in her brain." But her pitfalls of doubt almost did her in. By drawing me into a story within a story, she had convinced me that William Zinsser's *Writing About Your Life* could also guide me through such landmines. Zinsser's advice: "You must never forget the storyteller's ancient rules of maintaining tension and momentum." Carter's review had done that masterfully.

Wading When the Tide Is Out: Letters, Notes, and E-mails

While writing this chapter, I got an e-mail from one party in a troubled marriage on their anniversary date. Both spouses are friends. I held off responding; e-mails interrupt my writing. Yet the tension they create can distract—or deepen my writing process. I wanted to try out my contemplative skills. I didn't want to ignore the concern, but I wanted to avoid giving advice. How could I answer meaningfully but indirectly? A few days later, a tulip blossom provided a story-response:

> I hope you can pass the anniversary of this painful time with grace like our wounded poplar tree. Each spring it expands a tad, nearly absorbing the ringed gouge I caused by tying our dog's exercise line around the tree a decade ago. The offending nylon rope lies buried deep inside, but the tree goes on blooming. This morning my wife brought me a tulip blossom from it when she walked the dog.

The tension created by the e-mail drew me into a story of nature. (See resource 2, Multiple Intelligences as Spiritual Frames.)

Sometimes when life seems flat, you can intentionally jumpstart sparks of reflective energy by writing notes and letters.

When I was eighteen I started thinking about becoming a writer but as an undergraduate student and later as a graduate student in creative writing, I didn't really have a career as a writer so I wrote letters, sometimes as many as five or six letters a day. In looking back at the thousands of pages of letters, I realize those letters were how I practiced my writing.

Here Shawn Wong tells in the *Writer's Journal* how he created something out of nothing. When the tide is out, when there's not much to wade into, you can create your own wading pond. Ally with technology: practice the writing craft with e-mails, text messages, or blogs.

Letter writing can literally set a person free. The movie *The Hurricane* is based on the true story of Rubin "Hurricane" Carter, who was wrongfully imprisoned for murder in Paterson, New Jersey. Against great odds, Carter writes his autobiography from prison, but finally gives up on ever being released. Years later, an alienated American youth Lesra Martin, now living in Canada, finds his life changed by learning Carter's story.

Lesra starts corresponding with Hurricane in prison. That first letter was the first trickle that created a slow but irreversible wave of freedom. Finally, Lesra convinces his three adult guardians to leave their beautiful Canadian home and move down to a Jersey high-rise across from where Hurricane Carter is confined on death row. They choose to leave home to find home. They advocate for Hurricane, even when he no longer believes in himself, even when he rejects their help, even when self-styled militarists stalk them and threaten their sanity. The family's human belief in Hurricane functions like an icon of divine Love believing him into new life. Today Hurricane Carter is free.

Letters from prison comprise much of the Christian New Testament—especially the apostle Paul's epistles to churches he had planted. Paul affirmed, "My brothers and sisters . . . my joy and crown" (Philippians 4:1); chided, "You foolish Galatians!" (Galatians 3:1); and confided his vulnerable soul, "We despaired of life itself" (2 Corinthians 1:8). Paul claimed Christ's power is made complete in human weakness (2 Corinthians 12:9).

In his *Letter from Birmingham Jail,* Martin Luther King Jr. drew directly on Paul's example, an act so powerful it created a spiritual manifesto that turned the tide of the Civil Rights movement. Likewise, Dietrich Bonhoeffer, imprisoned and executed by the Nazis for opposing Hitler, expressed his most passionate hopes for the church's future in *Letters and Papers from Prison,* exchanged with his friend Eberhard Bethge.

Few letters create such life-altering legacies. But composing simple notes of affirmation, celebration, or concern can get you wading again into the script of your own heart (see exercise 13). I wrote this prayer poem as an e-mail note for a young person in a time of transition:

For Jeremy on His Journey

I pray that you are finding
some purpose and passion
in the direction of your life
that can see you through
the rough terrain and train
your inner self and soul
to hone your way and stay
focused on your destiny,
though you may know nothing
about it at all right now.

Sometimes I compose a bit of light-hearted doggerel, as in this wedding anniversary note:

Joel and Janie

Celebrate the joy of twenty!
Life with love is surely plenty,
spilling over into daughters,
echoing your song and laughter's
good medicine that keeps the heart
alive: Each step a brand new start.

Returning to Wade into the Wonder

I come back to wading again and again, even after learning methods for swimming (going far out), diving (going deep down), and floating (when the writing carries me). Especially after I've gone away and written into the flow for days, on returning I may only dawdle for weeks. But such playful dabbling carries me along inch by inch toward home, to wonder again.

In my journal, I wondered and pondered the lost sheep, the lost coin, and the lost son in Luke 15:

FOUND & LOST

Once I am found
I need to get lost
Again: in Wonder
Love, and Praise.

Later on some people will return to wading at an advanced level, a grown-up form of playing at the shoreline of conscious skill and unconscious flow — the image of surfing. For now we go on to master artful methods of swimming, skills for writing with a contemplative heart.

Tuesday Evening

Marin has progressed from a beach ball to trying out her doggy paddling skills and even crawling short distances underwater by scooping her hands toward her chest. Once she paddled underwater to find herself beneath a raft just when she needed to come up for air. She didn't panic. "I can hold my breath a little longer," she told herself. When she surfaced she was out farther than she planned. But Aguar swam over to meet her and the two raced each other to shore. In the afternoon they played with a beer can, filling it with water and throwing it in so the other would dive to retrieve it.

Exiting the water at the end of their day with hot sand shifting beneath their feet, they feel a bit giddy *and out of control. As they approach the beach umbrella they're whispering about going out beyond the big waves.*

Overtones of their conversation frighten Gram, who pretends to be finishing the last page of the novel she's been reading all afternoon. She's made up her mind. First, both grandparents must agree to fire themselves from this lifeguard job. Second, they must phone the parents about this dangerous talk of going out into the deeps. For that Marin and, yes, Aguar need advanced skills. Someone else with more expertise will have to show up on Wednesday.

 *EXERCISE 8*   ### Contemplating the Qualities of a Child

Imagine qualities of a child. Find the lyrics to the child's lullaby "Hush Little Baby." Have pen and paper ready. Sing, play, drum, dance, or listen to the song. Or listen to Yo-Yo Ma and Bobby McFerrin's version on their CD *Hush* as they joke around and counterpoint classic cello and pop styles. Give yourself some silence to contemplate childlike qualities. Then begin to write—or draw smiley faces, sad faces, or stick figures jumping, kneeling, or dancing. You might let a poem emerge. Find a way to name these qualities in a group, or with another person.

EXERCISE 9   ### "How Is Life Like or Unlike Kindergarten or Nursery School?"

Write this question on the top of a clean sheet of paper and put it away overnight. Then in the morning begin to write nonstop for ten to fifteen minutes. (For example, I never attended either nursery school or kindergarten. Now I joke that I'm spending the rest of my life catching up—learning how to play, how to use building blocks in relationships, how to paint and color with my fingers and figures of speech!) See where the question takes you. After reading over your essay, ask another person to read it aloud. Talk about the relationship of early childhood learning to adult learning and life.

Sounds and Silence

EXERCISE 10

Find a really noisy place, like a bench near a shopping mall or an expressway. Sit . . . observe colors, light, movements . . . close your eyes and slow down your breathing. Put your thumbs or index fingers in your ears for a few minutes (you will hear your own body's noises—or sounds like the ocean). Now release the thumbs . . . and try listening through the noise into the silence beyond the noise. See if you can hear faint sounds of nature (birds, insects, wind). Or perhaps you hear the distractions with new meanings.

Option: To practice the same exercise at home, turn up music loudly (inside or outside—but be considerate of your neighbors!).

Creative Memos

EXERCISE 11

Try placing scraps of paper or sticky notes with humorous messages or symbols of affirmation on a pillowcase, a steering wheel, or a vacuum cleaner—or under a coffee cup or a toothbrush glass. Or bake notes into cookies or bread. You can use fun notes just to surprise yourself—especially if you live alone—or as humorous reminders. (I draw teeth to remind myself of a dentist appointment.) How does it feel to tweak ordinary reminders with playful affirmations? Can you see longer-term value in everyday humor?

EXERCISE 12 — The Gift in the Struggle

Pause for a few minutes. See if you can recall an experience in your life (or in someone else's) where a gift emerged through a time of struggle, by surprise, with or without public recognition. Try writing about it as a story or poem. Find a way to share your story. In what way did the struggle give birth to a gift? What does this tell you about life?

EXERCISE 13 — Designing Your Own Notes of Celebration or Sympathy

Instead of preprinted cards to celebrate or sympathize with a friend, get one that's blank inside, or fold heavy paper into a card. Take several minutes to sit silently and contemplate the face of the person you're sending it to . . . memories . . . experiences . . . feelings. On a separate sheet of paper, use pen, pastels, calligraphy, or computer to write your own greeting, prayer, or affirmation. For a poetic format, try letting words or phrases flow down the page (or computer screen and print it). Using glue (or a glue stick to avoid wrinkles), affix your message inside the card.

Option: If you fold heavy blank paper to make the card, for the front side you might affix a photo—or design it on computer.

Chapter 3

Swimming—Focus on Methods

Reading life: luminous images,
simplicity of words and heart

Wednesday Morning

As the sun rises our two young friends are agog with high hopes. During the night Aguar's older cousin Vincente and new wife Valorie arrived for a surprise stay at Miguel's condo. Grandparents and kids are thrilled. Vincente, a grad student in oceanography, is training for the Olympics swim team. Valorie works as a marine biologist for National Geographic. With Vince and Val for coaches, Marin will make friends with the water. She pronounces she'll catch up to Aguar, who slaps Marin a high five and bets he'll still be ahead of her by nightfall. Each is a quick study and highly motivated: methods that start as mechanical movements will soon become second nature. Instruction will morph into intuitive skills. Just wait, you'll see.

If the metaphor of wading is play, then the metaphor of swimming is work. In Joseph Conrad's *Heart of Darkness*, the narrator says, "I don't like work—no man does—but I like what is in the work, the chance to find yourself. Your own reality."

In spiritual terms, the work becomes grace. There can be no *un*successful writing if it opens up the passion buried in the script of your unique Self. Good writing blesses the writer's soul. Then it will be good for the reader's soul.

When I read these lines to a group, one participant bristled at the word *good*. "You know I'm no good at writing—it's not natural. I was hoping this book would be different—that it would change my attitude." She stopped me in my tracks.

Later I told her writing that's good for me needs to do two things: affirm me *and* make me struggle.

With that she leaned forward, as if to answer her own objection, and said to the group, "You know sometimes it's good to do something you really stink at! I never liked art. So I've gone out and bought pastels and watercolors. Every once in a while I get them out and just scribble and smear around."

She got me thinking how I've never been good at competitive sports. I joke that I'm "athletically declined." Yet everybody needs some regimen of physical practices just to stay healthy. For me it's developed into a series

> *Each day, and the living of it, has to be a conscious creation in which discipline and order are relieved with some play and some pure foolishness.*
>
> —May Sarton
> *Journal of a Solitude*

of tai chi, yoga, and physical therapy exercises for my back (often now incorporated as prayer gestures). But every once in a while it's good for me to enroll in a class with experts; it makes me compete with myself.

Genuine Writing, Good Writing

Writing that's good is genuine: whatever validates your own life experiences yet also stretches you beyond what you know—to imagine what you don't know.

"So if you can't write, scribble!" I quip. Writing may not be your natural bent. But I'm offering methods for *transforming life*, not just skills for transferring information. Imagine creating your own multistranded lifeline, weaving content and contemplation, facts and feelings, instruction and intuition, all into a coherent, soulful experience.

Serious swimmers (musicians, artists, or scientists) sense their inner giftedness. Then they commit to the true grit of regular practice, honing their gift and giving birth to the passion already within. In spiritual traditions of East and West, three terms get used interchangeably for "methods," each with a special slant in the Greek New Testament: disciplines (*paedeia*—pedagogy), practices (*askesis*—ascetic), and exercises (*gymnastikos*—gymnastics). They function like scales for a musician or stretching for a runner. Writing methods are spiritual if they sharpen the eye of your awareness within and without, whether you are composing everyday notes or e-mails or formal presentations.

Create each day with discipline and order relieved with some play and pure foolishness, as May Sarton bids us. But unless we give serious attention to discipline we can't know the joy of relief from it.

You realize the burden of the gift and the gift of the burden. The title of one of C. S. Lewis's books, *The Weight of Glory*, conveys this paradox: one's greatest aliveness bears with it a heaviness of devoted practice. Whether tennis or writing, if you want to play life well, you decide to practice to let the gift come forth.

"The Swimmer Is One Who Has Learned the Nature of Water"

In my early youth I talked my mother into letting me quit swimming lessons (chlorine irritated my sinuses; I had lots of excuses). So my freshman year at Penn State I found myself in a required swimming class for physical education. During that blessed embarrassing experience I came across a metaphor that has guided me more than any methods I learned in the university pool: *the swimmer is one who has learned the nature of water.* I have never found the phrase in print. I think I heard it in a world religions class as a summary of Lao Tzu's ancient Chinese classic, *Tao Te Ching* — The Book of the Way. The Tao — what I would paraphrase as "the way" of paradoxical power — means yielding creatively to the fierceness and the gentleness of water, to the yin and yang in the ebb and flow of life.

The swimmer is one who has learned the nature of water. That single sentence still seems to embody the transforming mystery I find at the heart of spiritual traditions of East and West. It is the way of dying and rising, of weakness becoming strength. Losing

> *Swimming lessons are better than a lifeline to the shore.*
>
> —C. S. Lewis
> *The Weight of Glory*

oneself in a passionate cause unlocks the door to finding oneself.

Even little distractions may contain elements of the
big Way. The book you were looking for but can't find
leads you to a golden sentence you once marked in a
book you forgot you had. A phone call interrupts your
writing quandary, but in the synergy of the conversation a lightbulb clicks. To keep a pact with a friend,
you yank yourself from your desk and go to a movie:
you watch as your last bright idea blows up with a car
crash on the big screen; then without warning a new
one zaps you.

It just happened again. To keep a family pact intact,
I went to see *Stranger Than Fiction* and experienced the
Tao of death and resurrection. Harold Crick (Will
Ferrell), a perfectionist IRS auditor, begins to hear a
narrator's voice (Emma Thompson's) telling him he
will die. It sends him on a crazy journey that breaks
his steel-watch personality. While auditing a baker's
taxes, Mr. Crick tastes her freshly baked cookies, buys
a guitar on a whim, and falls in love with the baker.
Facing dying gets him really living. Then in one spon-
taneous moment Harold gives his life to save a child —
yet still lives on.

The serious stuff turns silly; the silly stuff turns serious. At every turn you meet Tao of life cresting and
crashing: the swimmer is one who has learned the
nature of water. The disciple is one who has learned to
find humor in the splashes.

I was given a similar lifeline of counsel and affirmation for writing. In her letter accepting my manuscript
Active Spirituality, the editor wrote: "Trust yourself to

26

WRITING   TIDES

speak with your own voice." I applied her one lifeline to myriad specific issues. It meant I didn't need to quote so many famous writers. I didn't need to mimic their styles (though that's an early part of any artisan's training).

On a practical level, her phrase still guides me: Write your heart out first; footnote later. On a spiritual level, writing in my own voice means disclosing my vulnerable stories as valued connectors—like my not learning to swim till I went to college.

Point of view is a primary vehicle for voice.

—Thaisa Frank and Dorothy Wall
Finding Your Writer's Voice

Finding my voice is a lifetime vocation, to link ancient and novel points of view. My work as a spiritual companion, teacher, and writer means helping people shift the position of the easel, to reframe the "what is" of life to see the "what can be."

Writing Methods as Spiritual Disciplines

Recently I cleaned the glass of my small office window that peeks out onto my wildflower garden. The essential self or the soul of each of us accumulates "smudge." In spiritual disciplines we encounter images of fasting, purging, pruning, emptying: stripping down the self to its essential core.

How can we connect this spiritual reality to the process of writing and vice versa? The swimmer knows to shed all but the slenderest bathing suit. Editors warn speakers and writers about the "fog index": in-house jargon and technical assumptions that clutter up the communicator's intent. The best of writing guides speak with one voice: simplify, simplify,

66

simplify. Witness William Strunk Jr. and E. B. White in the classic *The Elements of Style*.

> Omit needless words. Vigorous writing is concise. A sentence should contain no unnecessary words, a paragraph no unnecessary sentences, for the same reason that a drawing should have no unnecessary lines and a machine no unnecessary parts. This requires not that the writer make all his sentences short, or that he avoid all detail and treat his subjects only in outline, *but that every word tell.*

As you continue reading, I invite you to probe one central question for yourself: how can cultivating spare, vivid writing practices simultaneously tend to your soul's need for simplicity and vitality?

Simplify. Here are some basic guidelines to simplify writing so that each stroke of your pen or your keypad dips into the stream of the voice of your character. Practice using:

- Short words: hunt for crisp words like dig, speak, bark, stab; road, rock, star, trek. Avoid long, Latinized, or officious-sounding words.

- Short sentences: However, vary subject-predicate, singsong sentences by using connectors like "While . . . When . . ." Or use participles: "On returning . . . After exploding . . ."

- Short paragraphs: Break long sections into self-contained, sequential units.

- Strong metaphors and images: "shaft of light . . . valley of dry bones . . . days of wine and roses . . ."

- Strong verbs: "devour, jostle, thrust, rage, leap, slouch, soar . . ."

- Questions: anticipate readers' reactions; occasionally convert insights into queries: "How? Where? Who? What? When?"

- Stories: Tell a story first thing to begin a new theme; lead the reader inductively into an idea—rather than present a concept first and illustrate it with a story.

Prune. Get rid of extra verbiage. Let your writing come alive with action and direct experience. Aim to spawn insight from within that commits the readers to their new learning (like these exercises). Avoid using:

- Adverbs. Instead, pack the punch into strong verbs, images, and metaphors. Example: "She slammed the gate in his face" versus "She shut the gate angrily."

- Passive voice: "The broken back upended Jack's plans" versus "Jack's plans were interrupted by an injury." Exception: Use passive voice to convey a compliant attitude: "She was betrayed by her own apathy."

- The verb "to be" and its variants: Substitute action verbs. "As a researcher he never minced words" versus "He was a straightforward researcher."

- Flat adjectives. Delete or find a vivid substitute.

- A difficult sentence. After a timely effort to revise, trash it.

- Isolated fragments. Weave little pieces into a context; set up tension, then drop the morsel into the reader's mouth; use the fragment as a bridge following a story.

- Too many concepts: Season technical writing with multiple intelligences and stories; put pithy ideas or quotes into sidebars or epigraphs.

- Too much subjectivity. Season stories and memoir with a few concepts; for example, place a genius insight on the lips of a crazy character.

Spirituality and Punctuation

"A panda walks into a café. He orders a sandwich, eats it, then draws a gun and fires two shots in the air.

'Why?' asks the confused waiter, as the panda makes towards the exit. The panda produces a badly punctuated wildlife manual and tosses it over his shoulder.

'I'm a panda,' he says, at the door. 'Look it up.'

The waiter turns to the relevant entry and, sure enough, finds an explanation.

'**Panda.** Large black and white bear-like mammal, native to China. Eats, shoots and leaves.'"

The joke provides the title for Lynne Truss's best-selling book on punctuation, *Eats, Shoots and Leaves*. Here's a spiritual irony that sounds very Benedictine: how can you take something boring and get people laughing their way into doing something right? Tongue-in-cheek, I offer a spiritual punctuation guide for recovering perfectionists.

. Use the "full stop" of a period to stop readers in their tracks. Pause. Notice the tracks.

, "Never place a period where God has placed a comma," said Gracie Allen.

? Season your communication with **?** marks. Questions blaze the path to insight. Hmm, how can I convert this insight into a question? How can questioning the path lead to a new path?

; Balance a thought; drop the other shoe. Keep walking; I'll follow.

! Don't use lots of **!** points to tell me it's exciting! Excite the adrenal glands of my imagination with stories and images.

: Lead me deeper: from swimming to diving.

— Too many em dashes get me out of breath—better to sprint for such a long journey.

"" Don't they look like lovers? So practice "speaking the truth in love" (the apostle Paul). "Credit your quotations," he says. "Not too many," she says. Dialogue brings a dull idea to life.

' Don't let apostrophes creep in to your CD's or video's when videos and CDs work just fine. Does today's obsession with possessives mirror our addiction to possessions?

Multiple Intelligences buttress these methods and integrate left-and right-brain modes of learning. Scan your writing, speaking, and meetings for a quotient of linguistic/verbal, logical/mathematical, spatial/visual, rhythmic/musical, interpersonal, intrapersonal, naturalist, and existentialist forms of expression (see chapter 2 and resource 2).

Notice how John Fox's poem "The Marrow of Who I Am" draws on all nine intelligences and employs striking images and verbs to describe war's effects on families.

i.

I hear the sorrow of mothers
abruptly leave this world,
escaping into whatever sky is above the door
they open to solemn military men,
who bring bad news like an ancient Greek chorus.
Tears spill onto sofas
That do not matter anymore. . . .

ii.

The marrow of who I am
is a tree struck by the lightning
of anger and sadness, shattering
heartwood upon the earth. . . .

The marrow of who I am
is always creating new blood,
a life innocent to this world,
save in the mystery of forgivenesses home.

Word images leap off the page and take you into the room with the sofa and into the heart of the tree struck with lightning: pause and note the ones that arrest your attention. Then try your hand at practicing strong images (see exercise 14).

Why are these ideas of simplicity of words and vitality in speech so important? We live in a sound-bite culture. Subtle commercials, electronic billboards, and high-speed Internet images invade our psyches. Increasing numbers of younger folks (and many adults) have quirky learning styles or some form of attention deficit. Most people past middle age suffer some memory or hearing loss.

This very climate creates an opportunity to return to ancient forms of learning as in primal cultures. The rabbi, guru, or Zen master would teach by pithy riddles and parables. Genealogical data would be passed on via dance, drum, and drama.

Crisp images and verbs, memorizable phrases, and dramatic stories crack open the parched soul. They draw new life from hidden streams of consciousness, creating a new environment over time. They tap what Thomas Merton called "a hidden wholeness" in all things. The process is like Jean Giono's story of *The Man Who Planted Trees* in the barren regions of Provence, southern France. In the years between World War I and II, a shepherd goes about planting acorns into the ground with the point of his walking stick. Decades later the desolation turns into streams, groves, and villages.

The goal of this environment is the same for reader and writer: to draw meaningful connections that validate our experiences of success and failure and prod us for spiritual possibilities. Now we're back to the question I raised: *how can cultivating spare and vibrant writing practices simultaneously tend to your soul's need for simplicity and vitality?*

Fasting as a basic attitude. From these writing methods we can draw parallels for spiritual disciplines. Clutter is the opposite of simplicity; too many words and things detract from depth and focus.

Ignatius of Loyola used an expression, *Non multa, sed multum,* "not many, but much," loosely translated, "Less is more." When I go away for a praying and writing retreat, often I begin the first day with a simple juice and fruit fast (and continue the practice at lunchtimes.) Trimming down helps me wade back into the manuscript until I'm swimming in it again.

Fasting is not really about food or things: it is about cultivating the attitude of simplicity in all of life. This could not be more of a sermon to myself in this year when my wife and I are downsizing forty years of accumulated "treasures" in order to move into smaller quarters. Giving treasures to certain people makes the painful pruning process joyful. I want to live simply that others may simply live (see exercise 15).

"Not many, but much" leads to a sort of fasting from words. Befriending silences and walks around the lake function as downtime for incubation. Practicing an economy of words in writing and speaking can script one's psyche that less is really more. On one writing retreat, after a period of silence, I wrote this poem reminding myself to live my life message — simply, boldly.

Courageous Pauper

Paucity of words,
audacity in deed.

Fred Rogers of *Mister Rogers' Neighborhood,* an ordained Presbyterian minister, understood such simplicity. Prophetically breaking with television protocol, he would allow "dead air space," waiting for a child to tie a shoe or respond to a question.

I'm trying to create such holy pauses. While preparing an outline to lead a men's retreat, I glanced aside

to scan over the list of participants' names as my
prayer to keep the focus on people while preparing.
Then I set my handheld alarm for five minutes
(instead of my normal twenty) and began saying/
praying: "Be still, and know . . ." When a Mozart
sonata brought me back, in a flash I recalled a story
I hadn't told in years. In the margins of the yellow pad
I scribbled:

> * Cape.
> Tell story.
> Cod started
> kite tree.
> in the up
> I give up wind
> gust of wind (es)
> crashing m
> undertow
> paradise.
> of life
>
> JOURNEYMEN: APPRENTICES & MENTORS
> a. m.
> 9:00 Gather & intros.
> 9:30 Meditation (rock & water)
> (converse one/one →group)
> 10:00 How to integrate hard/soft?
> Aslan Lion: Gentle strength
> ⬆ Balance
> → Reach forward
> ← Draw back

In such ways I script my psyche: *Be still, and know . . .*
(something important that surfaces
in silence). I tell my soul to value
down moments like rests in a musical
score, like timeouts in the sports
arena (see resource 4, "Listen to
Your Soul's Code").

*[Writing] is work and
play together.*

—Anne Lamott
Bird by Bird

Balancing freedom and discipline. Oscillation in the swimming metaphor communicates this rhythm: the hand that takes hold must also let go of the water. Here we see the balance of learning methods and letting go of them, like the rhythm of breathing in and out. I find the same motto works for retreat leading and writing:

> Make a plan,   Learn the methods,
> Give up a plan.   Forget the methods.

The Möbius strip represents the single-heartedness of *discipline* and *freedom*: its two "sides" act as one. (Pause now and make another Möbius strip with these two words on it.) Healthy disciplines embody oscillating tides of solitude and solidarity, contemplation and communication, resting and risking, silence and speech.

I invite you to practice *free-flow* writing. Choose something light, something serious, something you'd like to explore, or some everyday experience. Just practice writing freely and spontaneously (see exercise 16).

A writer is not so much someone who has something to say as he is someone who has found a process that will bring about new things he would not have thought of if he had not started to say them.

—William Stafford
Writing the Australian Crawl

Now reverse it. Practice *disciplined* writing about something you know pretty well, in essay style, to cultivate structure and information. We say we're "swimming" in a subject, meaning it's really got us involved. It can be about your leisure experience or your professional expertise. Maybe it's health, money, faith, working, aging, or listening (see exercise 17).

Hard work versus surprise. Writing into life means learning to ride the Zen-like tides of discipline and freedom, working hard and getting surprised. So what does this have to do with spiritual practices? All you can do is prime the pump for some underground well of wonder to gush forth. You pant and sweat and break your back priming the pump.

Sometimes you write with breath, brains, and brawn and still no water comes. But if you're a writer, you never doubt there is water, even if you have to move your rig and drill another well. You leave that spot and start digging into another book. You start priming the pump again and look for that one gush of wonder.

A thing long expected takes the shape of the unexpected when at last it comes.

—Mark Twain

You work, you dream, you talk, you pray, you walk, you wait. But you do it all just for the sake of living awake. Then when something magic breaks through the chaos, it arrives as "effortless effort" in the ordinary work of science, sports, medicine, art, music, mathematics—and relationships. And you live awake for Love's sake.

Replenishing: reading, writing, and rhythm. You can't pour water from an empty cup. An early mentor gave me the golden lines, "If you want to write, write, write then read, read, read." Contemplation provides the overture and the reprise: notice, notice, notice—the rhythm that weds reading and writing with relationships.

Nothing is more important for the writing life and the spiritual life than to read. I mean learning to read all of life—as if worldly environments and your heart's musings and your neighbor's tales are books. You coach yourself into spiritual literacy by reading signposts written all around you—a luminous moment in nature, a line of a conversation, a mood created by music, a mesmerizing scene on TV, an art object that moves you beneath memory, a startling dream—a phrase on a page that stops you in your tracks.

For one thing, becoming a better writer is going to help you become a better reader, and that is the real payoff.

—Anne Lamott
Bird by Bird

We say of someone, "She really knows how to read the situation," or "He reads me like a book." A younger colleague paid this tribute to our mutual mentor who had died: "Rick knew how to read me and ushered me down the path."

The time-honored Benedictine method for reading and meditating with scripture (*lectio divina*) provides a transferable spiritual practice to sharpen our vision in reading and contemplating all of life.

The Practice of Sacred Reading

The scriptural *lectio divina* (literally, "divine reading") can be adapted to any text—poetry, fiction, or nonfiction—and to all of life. I propose a way to expand the *lectio* process and restore it to its original role of creating spiritual literacy in the tides of contemplation and action.

In the fifth century, Saint Benedict used an earthy metaphor of the *lectio* process: read a short text meditatively—"like a cow chewing her cud"—until you begin to "delight" in the presence of God. In the twelfth century, Guigo the Carthusian framed Benedict's *lectio* in four stages: reading (grazing); meditating (chewing); praying (ruminating);

contemplating (digesting, resting). The word has now become flesh in the reader.

You read until a short phrase or image in the text begins to lure you, or disturb you, and you follow where it leads. In the framework of this book's themes, we can think of the process of reading as *observing*; meditating as *wading*; praying as *swimming* and *diving*; and contemplating as *floating*.

Ignatius of Loyola's method of meditation adds the special use of imagination. In his early romantic life, Ignatius would read fictional love and war stories and visualize the scenes. Abruptly holed up in a Spanish castle after a serious leg injury, he used the same method with the Gospel portraits of Jesus and found himself drawn into the sights and sounds and characters in the stories. I liken the process to reading a text and then creating your own inner Hollywood set. I invite you to practice the *lectio* method on the ancient text of Genesis 1:1-3 (see exercise 18).

Ages before the ancient practice of *lectio* created a process for converting printed words into lived experience, it began as a process of converting experience into living words. First came Moses' vision of the burning bush, or the Buddha's childhood memory of sitting under the Bo tree. Then came the recorded story as a way to recreate the original experience for future generations.

As with the single edge of the Möbius strip, if you want to write your heart out, practice reading life. Contemplating a luminous image communicates to your soul, returning to contemplation; how you express yourself turns into communication again.

Jesus compared the luminous word that catches our attention to the image of seed: some falls on rocky ground, some on hard ground, some on good soil (see Mark 4:3-20). Cultivating our attentiveness and receptivity creates the good soil. Thomas Merton picks up this metaphor in *New Seeds of Contemplation:*

> *The surest way to arouse and hold the attention of the reader is by being specific, definite, and concrete.*
>
> —William Strunk Jr. and E. B. White
> *The Elements of Style*

Every moment and every event of every person's life on earth plants something in one's soul. For just as the wind carries thousands of winged seeds, so each moment brings with it germs of spiritual vitality that come to rest imperceptibly in the minds and wills of human beings. Most of these unnumbered seeds perish and are lost, because people are not prepared to receive them: for such seeds as these cannot spring up anywhere except in the good soil of freedom, spontaneity and love.

The *lectio* process creates a way to let seeds of love catch you, so that you can live and love purposefully and spontaneously, with discipline and freedom. Theologians like Saint Augustine and John Calvin speak of two books we are given—the book of sacred writings and the book of nature. This broader application of *lectio* pays serious attention to "Incarnation"— the divine word embodied in our most worldly experiences of nature and human nature.

Expanding *lectio* to reading life. The poet Jane Kenyon's vivid metaphor "the luminous particular" aptly describes both directions of the *lectio divina* process—to infuse the writing process with life and to draw life from reading all creation. Kenyon's aim in the lyric poem was to take a striking event or experience and craft it with such telling detail, crisp language, and physical imagery that the reader feels this.

Two examples put flesh on the ancient *lectio* method, applying it to "reading" all of life. In each case, like the poet Blake seeing "the World in a Grain of Sand," a single seed acted as a hologram to open the person's inner script to the world.

Born unable to speak or see, a young woman was determined to communicate. One day her teacher pumped and spelled w-a-t-e-r on her hand. Helen Keller wrote, "I understood that what my teacher was doing with her fingers meant that the cold something that was rushing over my hand was water," wrote Helen Keller. "There was a strange stir within me—a misty consciousness, a sense of something remembered." The mystery of language was revealed to her; one moment opened a new world.

An eleven-year-old was watching a news clip showing a homeless man sleeping on the street in downtown Philadelphia on a bitter cold night. Trevor Farrell insisted his parents drive him from their suburban Gladwyne home to the city that night. Ignoring his mother's plea merely to open the car window, he darted from the car to hand the man his own blanket and pillow. A single TV news clip had spread its roots in Trevor, until eventually his father quit his job and the family formed a nonprofit organization called Trevor's Place.

Life is filled with luminous particulars that want to arrest our attention and crack open the seed of our souls. Genuine insights come wrapped in awe. But awe can emerge from disturbance (as with Trevor) or hope (as with Keller) and often a paradoxical combination of both.

The key that unlocked John Fox's poem "The Marrow of Who I Am" dropped while conversing with a friend who commented on how sad and horrific the muddy, bloody Middle East war was, how senseless it felt. Stephen said, *"It hurts to the marrow."* One telling line now ricochets images that carry us to our own tear-stained sofas and lightning-split hearts.

The secret for staying awake to the sacred lines in all of life is the practice of recollection, harvesting "luminous particulars" along the journey.

Practice Recollection: Examen and Journaling

Swimming instills this back and forth rhythm as Søren Kierkegaard describes a life that must be lived forward, but can only be understood backward.

Sankofa, a primal symbol from West Africa, provides a graphic expression of Kierkegaard's thought. *Sankofa* portrays a bird with its feet facing forward and its head looking back, usually with an egg in its mouth. It reminds us to keep an eye on our primal past, to draw

> *If one looks long enough at almost anything, looks with absolute attention at a flower, a stone, the bark of a tree, grass, snow, a cloud, something like revelation takes place. Something is "given," and perhaps that something is always a reality outside the self. We are aware of God only when we cease to be aware of ourselves, not in the negative sense of denying the self, but in the sense of losing self in admiration and joy.*
>
> —May Sarton
> *Journal of a Solitude*

from its precious treasures, while moving forward into modernity. "Go back and fetch it" is a good translation. *Sankofa* echoes Socrates' words that the unexamined life is not worth living.

Picture this bird joyously dancing (or swimming) its way through life—feet forward, eyes backward, sideways, head forward again! Go back and fetch the essence of life. By practicing recollection, you can become this bird, harvesting the essence of life while moving forward on this swiftly tilting planet. You hear the bird singing in your heart, "If I hadn't gone through that struggle then, I wouldn't be prepared for this one now."

A simple form of examen adapted from Ignatius of Loyola's *Spiritual Exercises* provides a frame to practice recollection: notice the *gifts* and *struggles* in the daily grit (retroactive grace). Then ask: in light of what's going on, how is Life *inviting* me to move forward (proactive grace). Sometimes the invitation is to find the gift in the struggle.

Coupled with examen, keeping a journal allows the flesh of experience to become word; harvesting your journal allows the word to become flesh again. Experiment with this threefold framework (gifts, struggles, and invitation) to reflect and write on the events and encounters of the past day or period of time.

Try out these two practices, like twin training wheels for your bike, till you find yourself upright in heart, recollected in mind, and balanced in body again and again: keeping a spiritual journal (review resource 1) and practicing examen (see exercise 2).

Recollection means paying attention to the rhythms of grace. People say experience is the best teacher. But you can repeat the same experience without learning. Rather, experience reflected upon is the best teacher.

By paying attention to his emotional crisis in the 1920s, Chicago professor Anton Boisen rebounded to found what is now a global hospital chaplaincy movement. In his work, he referred to people as "living human documents." A "divine line" can arrest me while listening to another person open the documents of his or her life. It can also happen when I take time to listen to the documents of my own life.

At the end of August 2000, I noticed I was exhausted. I booked a personal retreat and a spiritual director at Kirkridge retreat center in Pennsylvania's Pocono Mountains. Without premeditating any structure for the retreat, I recalled my late friend and mentor John Oliver Nelson had founded Kirkridge in 1942, the year I was born. So I decided to take a walk on the nearby Appalachian Trail and reflect over my life from my birth to the present.

Aha! I would use the "decades" of the beads on a rosary I carry to pray over each year, one decade at a time—its gifts, struggles, and the invitation of each chapter as I looked back on it. It took two days. The third day ushered in the big question: *what is God inviting you to in the afternoon of your life?* I am still living into that quest.

Examining the tides of exhilaration and exhaustion promotes a healthy awareness of gratitude and vulnerability—while constantly asking, What's the invitation? Day by day, repeated methods of engagement and reflection function like the rhythmic oscillation of the swimmer. You keep writing and riding the tides.

I will
set sail
in the after
noon of my life
with thanks and
trust, love and hope,
on this journey home
again. What heaviness
I feel is ballast to balance
this ship en route to Destiny.

Wednesday Evening

It's been a day of deep breathing, scary experimentation, and incredible discovery for the two kids. By late morning, Vince and Val have trained each one separately in basic Olympic strokes—crawl, breast, back, butterfly, and side. The little duo start coaching each other, calling for time-outs, then acting plain silly.

Before noon all four take a break back at Miguel's condo. They watch Vince's Olympic intro swimming DVD, trying out gestures as they flail around on the floor. Partway into the diving section, Vince pauses it for a late lunch. After twenty-minute power naps, they sprint to a professional pool where they practice speed laps. Marin comes out ahead a few times. She feels irritated as she spies Aguar diving with older kids in the deep end. But with Vince's coaching she gets the hang of it too.

By late afternoon they make their way back to Gram's apartment where the whole gang celebrates Aguar's eighth birthday over pizza. After bragging nonstop, the two begin watching the Imax Coral Reef Adventure DVD Val brought. But exhilaration has given way to exhaustion. Marin slumps into her futon. Aguar wobbles back to the condo in Lolo's arms and crashes.

Strong Images: Observing and Practicing

EXERCISE 14

Read John Fox's poem "The Marrow of Who I Am" (page 71) twice. The first time read it aloud; the second time read it silently, underlining or highlighting particular words or phrases that speak to you—images that disturb you or lure you.

Option: Choose a striking image or metaphor from Fox's poem. Write the phrase on a clean sheet of paper. Take one minute to ponder. Compose a sentence using the phrase, and continue to write using strong verbs, gestures and metaphors (for fifteen to twenty minutes). Conclude with an ellipsis . . . Whether by yourself or in a group, read aloud.

EXERCISE 15 — *Simplicity as Fasting from Things, Experiences, Words, or Ideas*

To fast is to practice an attitude of simplicity. The Random House Dictionary refers to fasting as an "ascetic discipline," from *askesis,* "training" in Greek. But training is never for its own sake but always for a purpose: to sharpen one's mission (see chapter 5 and exercise 26). Periodic fasting, even from good things—food, reading, conversation, sex, work—can heighten one's appreciation and awareness. It's not hard to fast from luxuries. But since food is essential to life, every disciple can benefit from an actual food fast to experience a bit of God's suffering with poor people— and our hunger as spiritual hunger. It can be limited at first, such as a one-day juice fast. But it is always fasting and prayer, with the intention to offer the fast as prayer for a person or cause, and to open oneself more completely to God.

Free Writing—Cultivating Creativity (open style)

EXERCISE 16

I invite you to practice free-flow writing to cultivate freedom and spontaneity. It may be something lighthearted, something you're struggling with, or something you'd like to know more about. You might choose a topic from such everyday ingredients as dust, eggs, web, stone, roots, eyes. Since you are practicing freedom, just write till you feel finished.

Reflection: What parallels do you find with your intentional spiritual practices? What is the invitation in this chapter of your life: to more freedom? or more structure?

Disciplined Writing— Cultivating Structure (essay style)

EXERCISE 17

Practice disciplined writing about something familiar to you, as an amateur or as a professional, to cultivate structure and harvest information. Are you "swimming" in some topic or experience? As you develop the theme, you're writing an essay. It doesn't have to be a particular technical field (though if it is, try writing about it for an eight-year-old). Someone may be swimming in adolescent issues—as the young person, or as a parent or counselor trying to understand the stage. Another may be swimming in real estate—as an amateur looking for housing or a professional realtor. Maybe the issue is health, working, aging, faith, listening, speaking, or relationships.

Reflection: Ask yourself how your attention to this topic, of fasting or to the process of writing has created a spiritual lens to look at something going on in your life. Find a way to converse with someone else.

EXERCISE 18 — *Practicing* Lectio Divina *with Genesis 1:1-3*

I invite you to practice the Benedictine *lectio* method using the biblical text of Genesis 1:1-3 (below). Gently follow the process of reading (observing); meditating (wading); praying (swimming, diving); contemplating (floating). Do not try for specific stages; rather, read, reread, and ponder. If a phrase lures or disturbs you, begin to repeat it slowly with your breathing; if an image or metaphor emerges, visualize it; be with it. The word has now become flesh in the reader. The process may occur over a period of days rather than in one sitting.

> In the beginning God created the heavens and the earth. The earth was without form and void, and darkness was upon the face of the deep; and the Spirit of God was brooding over the faces of the waters. And God said, "Let there be light"; and there was light (AT).

Option: Try repeating the phrase "Let there be light," imagining various persons or problems, one by one, being bathed in light. (I do this with writing trouble spots.) With a group or a friend, you might each name concerns, and say it as a litany between each request.

Practicing Lectio *in Reading Life*

Take a minute to scan over a recent period of your life: conversations, chance encounters, books you've read, movies you've seen, places you've visited, dreams you've had. Allow a particular experience to surface, even if at first it seems quite ordinary. Sit for another minute in silence, simply being with that experience. Begin to write in whatever form it seems to take (free-flow, essay, poetry), but recall as many details as possible, without censoring any. At some point put down your pen or pencil, or pull back from the keypad. Read over what you've written and notice "luminous particular" phrases, metaphors, or images. Underline or highlight them. Read what you've written to someone, or have the person read it to you. Reflect a second time as you hear the phrases and images.

Diving—Focus on Depth

Practicing resiliency in spirit, mind, and body

Thursday Morning

Vince is up early watching springboard and platform diving, way beyond the elementary "hold-your-breath, jump-right-in, come-back-up" diving the kids saw at the pool late Wednesday. But at breakfast it takes no coaxing from Valorie to show the duo the wonders of underwater sea life. During the hour's drive to Pennekamp Coral Park they flip through the photo album of Val and Vince's year in Australia, where they met.

"We're here!" they shout, spying a sign, "Kids Practice Pool." Since Val's a certified trainer, she teaches basic safety of how to use the mask, fins, snorkel, and safety vest. Two big challenges are emotional (trusting your fear to the water) and physical (breathing through the mouth instead of the nose). Once suited up, they learn the mechanics of kicking the fins up and down from the hips and blast clearing the snorkel. Practicing in the kids' pool, they see a rainbow of tropical fish and replicas of a stingray and miniature dolphin. But Val will only be content if each can glimpse a few beneath-the-ocean bursts of real coral wonder—maybe this afternoon's snorkeling for children with basic skills.

I confided in a colleague group how hard it is to write while going through a major transition: in my case a move from my East Coast roots to Colorado. Someone said, just accept it. Then I heard myself say, "I think writing will save me from drowning this year!" In that instant I knew I *had* to write. A divine must. "Write as if you were dying." Annie Dillard's words rattled around in my head as I drove home.

I keep pondering a myriad ways this divine must shows up in small and great events. But always there's the connection between depth and death. You breathe in and out with the sense if you knew you were to die tomorrow, how would you live today? Yet it's really not about writing; it's about dying to each then to live fully into each now with gratitude and compassion.

Resiliency as Resurrection

Developing resiliency is as essential for diving as oscillation is to swimming. The core of Christian faith centers on the mystery of Jesus' death and resurrection, a resiliency we inherit in a living baptism. It is the way of paradoxical power — *Tao Te Ching* — the way that integrates the heights and depths of life into a continual flow of love. And that is the key: to bounce back with gratitude and compassion. Some people survive great tragedies but they become bitter and brittle.

When life is shallow, I need to plunge deeper. But when life plummets me to the ocean's floor, I need to mine the treasures of the deeps — and learn ways to bounce back. A swimmer begins by diving into the water (springboard diving) or within the pool (surface diving). But a moment of snorkeling or scuba diving opens a whole new world of beauty beneath the surface. As Psalm 42 says, "Deep calls to deep."

Do you ever look back at a project you completed and ask, *how did I ever do that?* But equally, do you look back to some experience and feel a twinge? *What was I thinking when I did that?*

"I carry two keys," says a rabbi. "The key in one pocket says, 'You are but dust and ashes.' In the other it says, 'For you the universe was created!'" To grovel in self-pity or gloat in self-importance is to endanger life's vital balance. Scientifically and spiritually, we are really stardust.

Diving takes us to razor's edge of the depths and heights. We understand Pascal's observation that nothing is more important than to know one's baseness and one's humility, and to know one's greatness and one's dignity. We write into and out of these tides.

We're back to two surfaces of the one-sided Möbius strip. If we try grasping for humility or greatness, we arrest the movement. But to recognize that both are going on at the same time is to live in a joyous rhythm of freedom and vulnerability.

We go up to Heaven and down to Hell a dozen times each day—at least, I do. And the discipline of work provides an exercise bar, so that the wild irrational motions of the soul become formal and creative.

—May Sarton
Journal of a Solitude

Just when we were thinking things were going swimmingly, life sends us plummeting to the depths for brief or prolonged times. We are handed a choice: learn to dive deeply, or quickly reappear at the surface and go on swimmingly. We can avoid the learning, cancel out the void. But how can we get back up when we're stuck or drowning because we've stayed down way too long?

Befriending the Void as Potential for New Life

Sometimes you choose to close a chapter of your life and enter a void where the new way is not fully formed. Other times a closing is thrust upon you: a loved one suddenly dies or disappears; a company goes belly up; a disaster wipes out life as you knew it. Or you are victimized but can't speak of it openly and have no choice but to stay in a toxic situation for some period of time.

Like a forest fire, old patterns get purged away, yet you see no signs of new life. Or like a drought, you awaken to realize your soul is parched. Transitions create a liminal space between known and unknown that can be the ripe place of gestation.

Twenty years ago I found myself in a vocational crisis. I felt unable to decide whether to stay or leave as a minister in a tradition-bound system. Wonderful things were happening in this community: new faces appearing in worship, new leaders emerging, and lives being transformed. Yet a small number of discontented people destabilized my spirit and kidnapped the community's vision. At that time, I knew practically nothing of contemplative practices that might have created a calm within the storm. There was one exception: I had been keeping a spiritual journal since my twenties, and that, I believe, saved my life.

One morning during this dark time, I recall turning to my wife at the kitchen table and saying, "If I don't preach nearly every week, something in me will die." What I innately realized was that the discipline of

writing and preaching created a lifeline of nurture for
my soul.

I did leave that church, and something in me did die. For nearly three
years, I inhabited the burned out floor
of the forest. I engaged in chaplain
ministry part-time to keep bread on the
table; it also kept my soul seeking
bread. I continued to keep a spiritual
journal, immersed myself in reading spiritual classics,
and engaged in newly discovered contemplative practices. Inhabiting the emptiness led to me to hear about
spiritual direction. A Jesuit spiritual guide crossed my
path. To nurture these budding shoots, I began training in spiritual direction.

> *The world breaks everyone
> and afterward many are
> strong at the broken
> places.*
>
> —Ernest Hemingway
> *A Farewell to Arms*

The emptiness I felt in leaving parish ministry led to
my gathering a small clearness group to discern my calling. I shared my initial ripples of finding and founding
an "oasis" in the desert of this aloneness. Following that
meeting I gathered a board and we founded Oasis
Ministries for Spiritual Development, a nonprofit organization to offer retreats and spiritual formation training.

Still, in the pit of my stomach I carried the void of
not writing and bearing a word of hope within a community. So I started to write about spiritual disciplines,
first for myself. Then I began to believe I had a message for other burned-out leaders and followers.

One night I awakened with a start: *I dream my computer catches fire. Afraid I have lost my writings I try dousing
it with water.*

Three years had stretched to five, and when I told
the dream to my new spiritual director, a Catholic

sister, she said, "It sounds like the burning bush to me." We thought the water might be the Red Sea, or Oasis Ministries.

Without a pulpit something in me had died. But a new pulpit had been born through my writing. By publishing a book, I would find the fledgling retreat ministry take hold in people and places far beyond the circle of any local congregation.

Yet I had many setbacks. Into a time of discouragement in writing and looking for a publisher, another tiny but potent dream appeared: *Jo Penn, who has terminal cancer, goes to seminary in Alexandria.* Ah, the "pen" of my writing would be the key to teach in theological seminaries and lead retreats. "Josephine," feminine of Joseph, was the muse to encourage the birthing of my new ministry. She was urging me to write today as if I would die tomorrow—and, like the third-century Egyptian writer Origen of Alexandria (on the edge theologically), to risk linking scriptural metaphors with contemporary life.

The timing with the editor of my first book, *Active Spirituality: A Guide for Seekers and Ministers,* came about through an unlikely resident at the retirement community where I served as chaplain. Ironically, she had a connection with the church conflict. We may discover our Teacher hidden in adversity.

I find a text in Isaiah (30:20-21) still speaking to me. "Yet your Teacher will not hide . . . any more, but your eyes shall see your Teacher. And when you turn to the right or when you turn to the left, your ears shall hear a word behind you, saying, 'This is the way; walk in it.'" We can freely turn either direction if, like the image of *Sankofa,* we keep listening to the voice from behind.

I have pondered how either way, had I stayed in a conflicted community or left, as I chose to do, the invitation was the same: to enter more deeply the void of uncertainty. Yet without engaging in spiritual practices I would have drowned. Either way, God's intent for me remained the same: to step back from mastery over any thing and yield to the Mystery in every thing.

Either choice could have plunged me to the depths to discover spiritual disciplines and allow a new form of community to emerge. We can get so obsessed about making the right choice that we miss the gift in either choice.

Something in me had to die for the acorn of my writing vocation to break open. My personal practice of journaling began to oak itself. While I was in the process of writing *Active Spirituality,* a colleague reintroduced me to the concept of *kenosis,* a frame or reference that would explain what had happened to me.

Kenosis: Emptiness as Space for New Life

All spiritual traditions have some concept of emptiness. It connects with the Hebrew Sabbath: to cease, to shut down our internal computers. If we fail to claim healthy soul space, life will hand us "sabbath" in the form of a car crash or a curveball, divorce or depression, debilitating illness, or vocational crisis. Spiritual practices of East and West would tell us: Do not wait for life to empty you. Learn to befriend emptiness as a rich source of creativity and courage.

The Bible's opening lines in Genesis read, "The earth was a formless void and darkness covered the face of the deep." But it is not a static void: "A wind from God swept—or brooded—over the face of the waters" just before the big bang when light exploded. Voilà! God spoke, or vibrated: "Let there be light!"

In the Christian story, the void at creation parallels the form of Christ's self-emptying (*kenosis* in Greek). "Christ Jesus, who, though he was in the form of God, . . . emptied himself, taking the form of a slave, being born in human likeness. . . . he humbled himself and became obedient to the point of death—even death on a cross" (see Philippians 2:5-8).

The idea of a necessary void preceding new life lies at the heart of kabbalistic mystical tradition of Judaism. *Zimzum* refers to the Creator contracting to make room for the creatures, like a jazz conductor stepping back so each player can solo. This stepping back creates *ein sof*, creative empty space where something comes out of nothing. The Jewish idea of *zimzum* and the Christian idea of the self-emptying God in Christ (*kenosis*) represent the crucial sacrificial aspect of God's ongoing creativity.

Here is the Mystery: If we inhabit our emptiness, we may find a treasure in the burned-out places of our lives, until, phoenix-like, the dark spaces become the next egg of creativity. As the ancient Hindu Rig Veda poetically states it, "Sacrifice is the navel of the universe."

This attitude of emptiness is countercultural. It sounds very Eastern yet is very Christian: *kenosis* means living out one's baptism, dying *and* rising in Christ. It means letting go of one's own preconceived

ideas—whether of self-inflation or self-deprecation—
then opening oneself to surprise possibilities.

The Buddhist experience of *Sunyata* as emptiness
and the *ein sof* of the Jewish Kabbalah draw Christians
back to our own truth: the self-emptying *kenosis* of
Christ is not only an event in history or a belief in our
head, but a daily "mind-set"—a moment-by-moment
experience in one's own history. We experience the
crisis of *kenosis* in three classic movements—the
release of attachments, the void of unknowing, and the
return to union with all created things. In writing and
life we can get addicted to the demon of our ideas
and certitudes.

Kenosis is a movement from the demon of controlling
(or being controlled) to yielding, from attachment to
detachment, from mastery to Mystery. It means shed-
ding the script "What do *I* want to do with my life?"
(or "What do *others* want to do with my life?" for many
women and minorities) to discover "What is Life inviting me to become?" We go through the void of silence
on the way to the invitation.

As a child of Western culture, I was taught to
view silence as a waste of time and spoiled experiences as "just so much garbage." Yet Jesus was
crucified on Golgotha, the town garbage pile, a
cosmopolitan waste heap. A Buddhist scripture says,
"As a sweet-smelling, lovely lotus may grow upon
a heap of rubbish thrown by the highway"—so the
disciple of the Enlightened One shines in the world.
Even wasted experiences and downtimes, when we
meditate on them in the present, can be re-deemed,
re-valued.

*Nothing in life is
wasted. Without
garbage we could not
have flowers.*

—Thich Nhat Hanh
Peace Is Every Step

Kenosis as "Negative Capability." In a letter to his brother dated December 21, 1817, poet John Keats referred to the state of unknowing as "negative capability." He tells how he was walking home from a Christmas drama with two friends. Keats describes one of them, Dilke, as a person who has "already made up his mind about everything": he would never learn anything new. In a moment of irritation, Keats's insight dropped in.

> Several things dove-tailed in my mind, and at once it struck me what quality went to form a man of achievement, especially in literature and which Shakespeare possessed so enormously—I mean *Negative Capability*, that is, when man is capable of being in uncertainties, mysteries, doubts, without an irritable reaching after fact & reason.

Next time you take a walk with an irritating friend or drop a note to a family member, marvel at this: you may play host to an explosive spiritual paradigm for generations yet to come.

Every creative person knows the void of unknowing as the womb for a new creation.

*An unanswered question
is a fine traveling
companion. It sharpens
your eye for the road.*

—Rachael Naomi Remen
Kitchen Table Wisdom

Novelists empty their own personality in order to enter the character they write about. Scientists may halt an experiment to let an idea ferment. Urging Quakers to free their slaves in the 1700s, John Woolman writes in his *Journals* how often his act of saying nothing in a Friends Meeting had more impact than words.

Emptying oneself into a cause. Sometimes you experience *kenosis* by immersing yourself in passionate action. You empty yourself of any attachments to consequences; you are free to act with love.

In *The Shawshank Redemption,* a movie based on Stephen King's novel, the character Andy Dufresne (Tim Robbins) is wrongly convicted of shooting his cheating wife and her lover. As prison librarian, he receives LP records. Locking the warden in the bathroom, Andy boldly enters the prison office and plays a Mozart duet over the sound system. Prisoners inside rise from sleep; outside they stand at attention. Red (Morgan Freeman) describes the music as "so beautiful it can't be expressed in words, and makes your heart ache because of it . . . It was like some beautiful bird flapped into our drab little cage and made these walls dissolve away . . . and for the briefest of moments—every last man at Shawshank felt free." Then Freeman's voice announces that Andy "got two weeks in the hole for that stunt."

Genuine humility means following your passion to bless people—like Gandhi, King, or Rosa Parks. Love frees you to claim your gifts and risk being thrown into a dark hole.

Dark Night of the Soul and Depression

I'm learning to befriend silence and emptiness to free myself from things and open myself for courage and creativity. But "blessed are the poor in spirit" is never an easy blessing whether by choice or circumstance. For me, writing into the tides of my own bipolar disorder is one such difficult blessing.

Dark night of the soul is not the same as psychological depression. Depression's sources vary from an innate chemical imbalance to outward life crises like abuse, death, divorce, or acute disappointment in oneself or others. Therapy can help—so can medications, like a cast for a broken bone or insulin for diabetes. But I believe a spiritual lens on this ambivalent blessing is not a luxury but essential to staying vital even when sad.

A student asked her therapist, what would be the difference between depression and dark night? The counselor paused—then said, "The outcome." One person may enter a crisis with no recovery. A second may go through a vocational or marriage crisis, then find a new job or a new relationship and recover functionally, yet with no apparent spiritual transformation. A third may go through the same events and undergo a spiritual transformation hidden in the night of crisis.

For still others the transforming night arrives unbidden and unrelated to any innate imbalance or outward crisis: constellations of meaning and beauty come together serendipitously. For each the promise is the same, as God speaks through Isaiah: "I will give you the treasures of darkness and riches hidden in secret places"(Isaiah 45:3).

That treasure is love, even when I despair for want of feeling it. "Depression is the flaw in love," writes Andrew Solomon in *The Noonday Demon: An Atlas of Depression*. "To be creatures who love, we must be creatures who can despair at what we lose, and depression is the mechanism of that despair." Those demons have visited me.

NOON DEMONS

These demons sneak in at high noon:
   Just look at what you've done!
Are they handing me
accolades or accusations?
   Look at your success!
   You'll never top that, fat cat.
   Look how you messed up!
   You can't walk the talk you talk.
Either lie will do.
   How dare you speak another word!
I quit and brood.

Ah! A whole new nest
of creatures sprout their wings.

Kenosis creates a pause, the meaning of *Selah* in the Psalms. Writing about pausing calls me to pause again . . . After some silence, I wrote in my journal: *I'm revising chapter 4 and being revised myself, revisioning who I am. I come again as a child to the first day at the beach: simple attentiveness to what is changes what was—and what will be.*

Depression and anger. I can never forget Mary's "teaching" in the wake of riots and assassinations in the late 1960s. Recruited from the streets of Westside Chicago to educate us minister-types for urban ministry, Mary would say, "Apathy is frozen rage." Like a liturgical refrain during this month-long program when anyone recounted a surprise incident of violence, we would hear it again: "Like I say, apathy's just frozen rage."

That fall I took a course on The Psychology of
Education at the University of Chicago from Allison
Davis, author of a classic series on descendants of
slaves, *The Eighth Generation*. (I recall my delight two
decades later when he was featured on a Black
Heritage postage stamp.) The class could be summed
up in Davis's repeated phrase: "Depression is anger
turned inward." It sounded only a tad more scholarly
and Freudian than Mary's refrain; I was sure the two
had colluded.

Writing *into* depression calls me back to attention
like the child mesmerized by the ocean. I notice two
things: First, often I find anger beneath the depression,
and anger is energy. Apathy's spell is broken; I can see
depression as negative capability. Second, I feel
depressed because I feel out of sync with the world,
like many creative people—probably you who are
reading this. Negative capability again. Seeing oneself
as a misfit can release energy for good: witness Jesus
and a host of misfits in his train—from Mary
Magdalene to Saint Francis, Van Gogh to Mozart,
Martin Luther King Jr. to Mother Teresa. Lonely pilgrims draw courage from other sojourners.

Writing *out of* depression conveys twin meanings:
writing your way up and out of depression, and writing out of the bottom of depression's well while still in
it. We always want the first, but it really helps to have
a mentor to validate the second: you can keep scrib-
bling around at the bottom of the well.

Abraham Lincoln suffered serious bouts of depression, even suicidal talk, as Joshua Wolf Shenk reminds
us in *Lincoln's Melancholy*. In 1862, amid demoralizing

military calamities, Senator O. H. Browning entered Lincoln's library despite instructions to not disturb the president, and found Lincoln writing. The president looked terrible—weary and troubled. Taking his friend's hand, Lincoln said, "Browning, I must die sometime."

"However," Shenk writes, "one crucial detail upsets such a simple picture: Browning found Lincoln *writing*." Lincoln was doing the work that saved him from despair: work that became a compass to guide the nation then and in future generations.

Ultimately the conversion process of seeing so-called negative emotions as capability is not something we do at all, but a transformation worked in us. We can claim Saint Augustine's wisdom: "Hope has two beautiful daughters, Anger and Courage: anger that things are the way they are, courage to make them what they ought to be." Writing and spiritual practices befriend the soul's desire for transformation (see exercise 20.)

In the film *The Matrix*, Thomas is transformed when he begins to doubt the dehumanizing matrix surrounding his work. His anger at the system then causes him to listen to the (phone) call to freedom. We are blessed when we begin to discover the gift of negative capability in times of doubt, confusion, and anger, moving us to contemplate a new sense of call. Even prolonged periods of frozen rage can begin to thaw in the light of awareness and yield the fruits of understanding and compassionate courage.

> In a real dark night of the soul it is always three o'clock in the morning, day after day.
>
> —F. Scott Fitzgerald
> *The Crack-Up*

I get surprised by goofy gifts in my down periods. Driving back from lunch I confided in a trusted colleague, "Art, I'm sorry I wasn't a very good conversationalist today—one of my down times." "I like you better this way!" he jibed. When I am not so full of myself there is more space to listen.

"The opposite of depression is not happiness but vitality, and my life, as I write this is vital, even when sad," concludes Andrew Solomon in *The Noonday Demon*. "Every day, I choose, sometimes gamely and sometimes against the moment's reason, to be alive. Is that not a rare joy?" I can taste that joy now.

I got into Evelyn Underhill's masterful volume on the history of Christian mysticism one snowy New Year's day. I came away with this thought from the mystics regarding sufferings—psychological, spiritual, or physical; plagues, demons, or wars: *until you are freed of the affliction, let it be a summons to pray*. To pray is to yearn, and writing is a way of yearning.

Debilitating Silences as Gestation and Generativity

In her thirties Willa Cather got the courage to send Henry James, her much-admired mentor, a copy of her first book of short stories, *The Troll Garden*. The story goes that James never responded. When a mutual friend urged James, he wrote back to the friend castigating Cather as a female and her fiction as promiscuous—even admitting he hadn't read it. Still, he promised the friend he would get back to Cather. He never did.

Cather was handed James's putdown. Her mentor's scorn and nonresponse cast a spell of shame on the gifted author. For five years she hid *The Troll Garden*, even refusing to show it to a friend, and wrote only dribbles that she deplored.

The spell was broken when another mentor, Sara Orne Jewett, validated Cather's Nebraska regional "reality" as worthy material for art. The floodgates opened, and Cather would give the world the literary treasure *O Pioneers!* followed by *My Antonia* and a host of other works.

Maya Angelou's poetry gushed forth only after a prolonged period of self-chosen silence in response to being shamed. Works of art lie gestating in a void of silence. We are sometimes literally "dumbfounded"— speechless for brief moments or long periods, like Isaiah after the king died, or Zechariah after hearing a birth announcement. The two words call us back to the true self: "Dumb" speaks of our being silenced, emptied—*kenosis, ein sof, Sunyata*. "Founded" speaks of a new plane of existence, a new foundation for our life.

I learned firsthand about such debilitating silence during the three-year period when I said something in me would die without a pulpit. Now, blessed with the tincture of timing, a stroke of a key on my laptop can strike a match in me and set this new pulpit ablaze.

Writer's block as invitation. Sometimes writing is like the Frank Sinatra CD my wife tried to play. It got stuck on a phrase "this longing for you" and refused to budge. I had to use my CD cleaning pad twice before Old Blue Eyes would move on to crooning about night and day. I long to move into the message I know lies encoded in the grooves of my brain and crevices of my heart. But it won't budge. I can dawdle over the same phrase for hours.

For days I contemplated this tiny experience with the CD. First, I thought, I need to trust that the script of my genuine longing actually *does* lie buried within me. Second, I need to clear away the debris that hides my awareness of it (Monday's theme at the beach). Third, as a type A personality, I need to reeducate myself in the virtue of patient pauses to get in touch with my longing for Love and my love of words.

Our places of impasse may seem as minor as the stuck CD or loom so large we feel paralyzed. By paying attention to ant-size obstacles and harvesting a bit of spiritual learning, we train the eyes of the heart for elephant-size ones (like when something in me died for three years).

I just experienced an ant-size block. I couldn't write the vignettes for our two kids preparing to dive. Legally a child must be ten years old to train for scuba diving (Self Contained Underwater Breathing Apparatus). How could I get a seven-year-old to dive to the bottom of the ocean and see the coral? Part of diving is delving into the research. I spun my wheels for huge chunks of time. Then it struck me: *You feel inadequate to write about swimming and diving.* So I went online and found a beginner's Olympic manual. I contacted a diving training center in Little Rock, Arkansas, and another in Lancaster, Pennsylvania. (I'll let you in on a secret: at 5:32 p.m. one evening it occurred to me: I could have her *dream* she is diving.)

Getting diving information thawed my paralysis so I could write again. Yet I couldn't have told you the reason. The revelation "that's why I couldn't write that" is as blessed as the urgency of writing it when at last the idea surfaces in my line of sight. It teaches me patience in the next exasperation. But equally important is exploring the reason for the block. Writing into an obstacle can pierce a pinhole into a universe of black holes where stars are waiting to be born.

Sail forth—steer for the deep waters only,
Reckless O soul,
exploring, I with thee, and thou with me,
For we are bound where mariner has not yet dared to go,
And we will risk the ship, ourselves and all.

—Walt Whitman
"Passage to India"

E. L. Doctorow is sitting in his study in New Rochelle, New York in 1972, unable to write. He can only stare at the wall. So he starts writing about the wall. Then he writes about the house the wall is attached to—a three-story brown shingle with dormers, built in 1906, the start of an optimistic new century. President Teddy Roosevelt has just sent the U.S. fleet around the world. Women carry white parasols; men wear white skimmers. It's a cozy self-satisfied America, where African Americans, Native Americans, and immigrants are invisible. In Doctorow's imagination the wall explodes into a whole new multicultural world that we know as a book and a musical, *Ragtime*.

The wall became a link to creative imagination. In *Gravity and Grace*, French worker activist Simone Weil speaks of the Greek concept of *metaxu* or bridge: how the barrier may become a passageway as prisoners tap out codes using the walls of prisoner-of-war camps. I invite you to try writing into an obstacle in your life (see exercise 24).

We are trained to destroy whatever gets in the way of what we think we want—nations, things, nature, people—as if they were devils when really they may be angels of annunciation. Doctorow could have changed his seat; instead he wrote into the wall.

Writing into not writing. After a wounding church situation, a single African American pastor found herself unemployed and living in a borrowed room. What is our calling when we don't have a call? She determined to write a sermon every week even though she had no one to preach to. Paying attention to the empty period and writing into it kept her spiritual connection vital. When she got another call, she had been healed by her own unpreached sermons, readied for a fresh start.

Writing about not writing. During a praying writing retreat at the Daylesford Abbey near Philadelphia, I awakened at 5:30 on a crisp winter's morning and fired up a wood stove in the cozy hermitage; the sunrise ushered in a golden day. Then I sat till late morning in front of my laptop's blank screen. But somehow I remembered the advice: *be gentle on yourself; befriend the void.* I began tapping into these lines:

WRITER'S DELAY

Today I pray that this delay
in writing (am I fighting or inviting
it?) will be the gift to sift
the gold from new and old,
providing space for grace
that integrates new insights.

Writing *while* not writing. When I'm really stuck I ask myself, *what would it mean to inhabit my longings?* Dried up dreams provide valued clues. Like moose droppings in Alaska, if all you have is excrement, keep on sleuthing and eventually you find the moose—and the muse.

So I sleuth the moose tracks. Sometimes I'm stuck because I don't have a home (a publisher) for what I'm writing. Then I keep writing my way home to my true self and the Truth at the center of the universe.

Other times, like Noah building the ark and praying it's going to rain, I go right on building the ark: I tell myself it isn't the season for rain, yet. Then when floods come (a publisher says yes), my whole body, breath, and brains spring with adrenaline. But the waters recede and I'll feel paralyzed with all the rebuilding. That's when I need to remember: *you're writing while not writing.*

> In the drowsy dark caves
> of the mind
> dreams build their nest
> with bits of things
> dropped from day's
> caravan.
>
> —Rabindranath Tagore
> *Fireflies*

While writing this I've pondered how I told my colleague group the truth: that it's nearly impossible to write during a major transition. But here is my gospel course on miracles: just tell God something's impossible; then when it's finished, you've got your miracle! By relinquishing the impossible work, when it arrives it is pure gift. In the between time, just keep writing and trust a greater truth: *you're writing inside the next egg of creativity.*

Or if nothing comes, you crawl inside the next egg again, and that's another miracle. Once I had nothing to write so I wrote about that.

Writing Nothing

I write about
Nothing.
No thing.
Ah! No thing really
matters,
only relationships.

Absence morphed into presence, nothing into everything. I yearn to live this truth.

Two decades ago if you asked me what creates writer's block, I would always answer: fear of rejection. Now that I know it's not so simple, I just try to be with what is—whether moose manure or amazing coral: each inhabits the low places.

Once while on my knees to look at a tiny fern, I recalled William Stafford's image that you have to kneel down to discover poems; that's why successful people rarely find them. You write into the universe when you get down close to the ground of humanity. A scientist finds new ideas by dropping beneath "facts" into the rich humus of doubt. One way to deal with writer's block if ideas fail to come is to lower your standards and get surprised by whatever comes along.

Kneeling down for truth parallels the spiritual truth that the Messiah hangs out with the lowly and the marginalized—whether dirt poor or filthy rich—and in the marginalized parts of your own psyche. Rudyard Kipling said that if you want to write, take care not to drive the poor from your doorstep. Staying close to the poor or the poor in spirit keeps you close to your own writer's edge.

"Diving into the Wreck." "How's the book going?" a colleague asked. I said, "I'm into the chapter on writing as diving, and I'm in over my head." She asked did I know Adrienne Rich's poem "Diving into the Wreck"? She then recounted her own story of scuba diving with a trained professional to view a Civil War cannon. "I was afraid a lurking snake might bite me. My guide had to push my hand three times before I would touch the cannon. The moment I did all my fears evaporated." Touching her fear freed her.

After we talked, I raced to my den. With a few deep breaths, I went online and found Rich's poem. I could feel the poet plunging into the wreck of a woman's life using ancient myths as her scuba gear: words become her Global Positioning System. But she never loses sight of the object: to experience the wreck, not facts about somebody else's wreck.

Connecting rusty links of my afternoon's unbidden research, I felt my spirit hoisted out of the rubble of defeat into delight.

I found my buried program notes of the night Penn State researcher David A. Bright took his audience (via computerized theatre) to join his voyage down to the *Titanic*. He told us how *Titanic* treasures have been pilfered so that international rules now guard a fragment of crystal or a rusted penknife. An abandoned wreck may contain priceless treasures. Yet the beauty of the dying coral reef may create sadness. Treasures in wrecks; sadness in beauty: I was writing nonstop. I was late for dinner.

> *All good writing is swimming underwater and holding your breath.*
>
> —F. Scott Fitzgerald
> (letter to his daughter)

Diving into the fear. It's true that fear lies at the root of most poor writing. What makes for inferior writing is being afraid of one's interior core. Fear-based writing is coated with affectation: a fearful writer uses loads of *italics*, exclamation points, and drops adverbs *profusely*, afraid you won't get the point! Unsure of one's own voice, a timid writer resorts to big words (like affectation!) and run-on quotations.

Yet that's where we often start; I did. Scratch the coating, and you begin to find what's real.

Now try turning the phrase on its head, like an Eastern koan: Fear is at the root of most good writing.

I have spent my life surrendering to the experience of going down into the dark of the writing process.

—Joan Chittister, O.S.B.

You break fear's hold by diving into it, by going down into the barrier reef: that is where you find the coral that's real.

In 1985, Joe Simpson and Simon Yates, fit, skilled, and confident, scaled the daunting 21,000-foot Siula Grande in the Peruvian Andes. The movie *Touching the Void* chronicles their real-life expedition. On their way down, Joe loses his footing, falls and shatters his leg, driving the fibula through his kneecap. For a while Simon tries to save Joe by tying two ropes to let him down by 300-foot increments. However, convinced that Joe is dead and he, too, will surely die, Simon is forced to cut the rope and the injured man zooms into the rocky void. The rest of the story takes us to Joe's incredible crawl-by-crawl, breath-by-breath trek back to freedom and life.

Resistances invite me to dive into the void of my worst fears. Whenever I find myself holding back from

a challenge that clearly taps my passion and gifts, it's
usually not about my overbooked calendar. No, the
root resistance is failure to trust my own worthiness to
give voice to my experience. Writing provides the
scuba gear to go into the deeps.

Sometimes you can script yourself with methods to
cultivate depth. Return to wading and wonder by playing with words, toying with ideas. Writing in free-flow
style can release dammed up creeks of the soul (see
exercise 16).

Or try the opposite: engage in some structured
forms that require discipline, such as haiku. In a group
Rob and I used to attend together, he often got teased
for using a fountain pen. Years later, the same thing
happened in another group. Responding to the teasing,
his friend e-mailed him a haiku that he forwarded to
me—a humorous reminder of our good times.

> The impression made
> From the tip of a fountain
> Outlasts an e-mail.

I ponder how the haiku picks up the playful teasing,
yet gives it depth. True to form, the second line contains a reference to nature, or spring. I
notice how the 5-7-5 syllable structure
draws on linguistic, mathematical,
rhythmic, spatial, kinesthetic, naturalist, and existentialist intelligences—and
exemplifies the interpersonal and
intrapersonal ways we learn from life
(see exercise 21).

*Poetry is delicious; the best
prose is that which is full
of poetry.*

—Virginia Woolf
The Common Reader

Writing a poem in the form of a sonnet calls forth even more complexity and depth, coupling analysis with emotion. Shakespeare's Sonnet 116 provides a beautiful example of fourteen lines grouped in three quatrains (four lines each) and a concluding couplet (two lines). To enter the nuances of this highly structured poetic form can function as a disciplined distraction—gymnastics to unite head and heart (see exercise 22).

Writing a prayer in the form of a "collect" offers a simpler way to create depth and brevity at the same time: an opening address to the Sacred One (choosing a meaningful metaphor or name for God), followed by a descriptive phrase, then a request with a purpose—and finally a concluding "signature" line (see exercise 23).

Prayer is a dive . . . It is bold impulse, pure throw of yourself into the unknown, and the premeditated, intentional methodology . . . We pick up the prayer book, hold the rosary, determine what it is we want to ask or thank God for on this day. And yet, for all our planning, we still have to leap.

—Lindsey Crittenden
"The Water Will Hold You"

Practicing Resiliency

The whole spiritual life is about developing resiliency with love. Love is what makes for spiritually effective writing: love of words, love of ideas, love for your subject, love for people thirsty for your life-giving words.

Falling in love with words is the key to every form of writing as falling in love with the water is the key to every form of diving. Thursday's diving takes Wednesday's swimming methods to go down deep, breathe underwater, then come back up for air. The key is not just to bounce back but bounce back with joyful compassion. Writing can keep you buoyant and regenerate love for an exhausted spirit. Practices for resiliency emerge out of your unique life experiences of crisis and hope.

My first writing crisis happened at Princeton Seminary in 1967. I had elected a two-course credit master's thesis my senior year. One January morning, four months before I was to graduate, I recall staring at my poorly organized files, convincing myself I would fail the thesis and not graduate. I talked to my adviser, Professor Bruce Metzger, realized there was no turning back, and decided to immerse myself in the challenges. When, to my surprise, the thesis received the Prize in New Testament, it had become a thesis of my life: to plunge myself into the challenge and find the treasure at the bottom of the abyss. The nest egg of that prize became the financial incentive for a life-changing doctoral program in the city of Chicago. But the real prize, then and now, comes in the spiritual learnings in the struggle and in offering those gifts to the world.

I see a pattern in my life story: I take an initial risk, but partway into the project I feel overwhelmed. Then I rise again. Does this happen to you? It can happen to me as surely while rehabbing my deteriorated front door or launching a new ministry program. I get easily seduced into thinking an expert should do it.

It has happened again as I wrote this chapter. A voice accuses: Who are you to write about resiliency of spirit when you sit at this keypad for hours, hands frozen, brain on ice? But another voice affirms: Who but you should write this chapter? How could you

> *I'll believe computers can think when you ask one a question and it replies, "That reminds me of a story."*
>
> —Gregory Bateson
> anthropologist, cyberneticist, linguist

write of ways to restore confidence if you didn't struggle to regain it?

I was talking with a younger colleague whose diving expertise I envy. He was telling me how he gets the greatest joy while coming back up from a deep dive, holding his breath and being drawn toward the light. Transfer this to writing. Imagine it.

Try these nine tested components for your spiritual scuba equipment. Or imagine them as rungs on a cosmic ladder where angels ascend and descend.

Storying. Stories transmit the oxygen of hope. I use story as a verb because stories are dynamic; they refill the storehouse. In preaching I talk about "storying the sermon," oxygenating your ideas. Fiction is stories. But nonfiction needs stories too: when you find yourself riding high on an idea, pause to let the words become flesh. Aim for newscaster Edward R. Murrow's phrase "You are there," so readers see themselves in your forest of words, ideas, and images.

LOOSE GOOSE

The muse is on the loose.
Ah, she is the Wild Goose,
and her egg of gold
is in the story told.

Mentoring. Where have all the heroes gone? We have a hard time finding mentors not just because they have feet of clay—they always have. But in our time no elder can say, "This is the wisdom you need"—because no one has ever been an elder in the twenty-first century before. You can bypass this time warp and cultivate resiliency by carrying on an imaginary conversation with mentors who've crossed your path (see exercise 25).

Researching. Delve and dive into your subject matter for love—whether physics or philosophy or psychology or geography. By immersing yourself in the grit of it, you find the luminous particulars as you come back up for air.

While writing *From a Buick Eight*, Stephen King took over a week to delve into the on-the-beat habitat of Pennsylvania State Police troopers in off-the-beat counties outside Pittsburgh. King didn't travel there to provide geographical facts but to create an environment so the driverless car seems real though surreal.

Delaying. In 1933 George Gershwin finally got a contract to adapt Edwin DuBose Heyward's 1925 novel *Porgy* as an opera, collaborating with his brother, Ira, and Heyward. Despite the contract, Gershwin took the summer of 1934 to go down with Heyward to the Carolina barrier islands and Charleston's Catfish Row to experience the rhythms and blues of people on the edges of survival. Out of that delay came a new form of American opera about a poor black man named Porgy and his lover, Bess. Depth was born by moving away from the full cup of success and learning from beneath. Investigation becomes incarnation.

Conceptualizing. Ideas and concepts like *kenosis* and Keat's Negative Capability anchor my swaying bipolar ship till I'm ready to leave port again. The Multiple Intelligences open me to writing with my whole body: when I find a home for a pet idea in my manuscript I clap and shout (till my Sheltie used to join in—ah, now he's gone); I do the math with my page numbers and word counts, and I sing the blues. I absolutely trust the idea of writer's block as spiritual conception—though some pregnancies are frightfully unpredictable. Concepts script the psyche: when an editor sets a time limit, for me it's not a deadline—it's a due date.

Retreating. I resonate with the frequent writing getaways Annie Dillard describes in *The Writing Life*. Periodic retreats get me diving into my soul and self and let the script in my own heart unfold (see resource 4, "Listen to Your Soul's Code").

RE: INCARNATION

This writing's fresh:
It's flesh made words
and Word made flesh.

Outlining. Like scuba diving gear, a well-developed outline saves me from self-destructing with a dearth or an overkill of ideas. But, I tell myself, if in the writing process your character changes (you or your fictional creation), scrap the plan. A die-hard outline can strangle a living organism.

OUTLINE FRIEND

Make an outline,
Put away the outline.

If the outline returns,
let it be your friend
and not your master.

Computing. Click "Save As . . ." and give your document a slightly new title, then ruthlessly prune, prune, prune. In *Titanic* language, you knock off the barnacles, cut the ropes, and take away the treasures.

Editing. Move text around. To keep from adding new text while writing this book, I began skimming with my mouse. Suddenly, a big chunk I had written for chapter three seemed tailor-made for the topic of depression in chapter four. I proclaimed aloud, "I didn't know I wrote that for this!" It happens often. But deleting text is hard; it's been called "killing your darlings." After exploring the deeps, I prefer a more playful metaphor:

FINAL EDIT

Some favorite pets
I must get into this circus
to bring people back
to the child
of their hearts.
Others will have
to wait for another show.

Thursday Evening

The glass bottom boat ride faded compared to snorkeling a few feet above the coral reef: an iridescent world had opened in the kids' faces—azure, amber, crimson twisty creatures frolicking, dancing, kissing in the sunlight. After they get a bite to eat at Pennekamp, sleep trumps excitement on the trip back. In twenty minutes Aguar snaps awake to play electronic games. Marin's lost in a dream: in it she's a marine biologist—all grown up and scuba diving among exquisite coral and anemone, checking for decay. It seems someone else is photographing behind the scenes. She awakens with her head spinning and too groggy to tell anybody.

Finishing ice cream back at Gram's apartment, Marin gets a text message from her mom and step-dad and Aguar phones Miguel. The two are ready for a sleepover at Miguel's condo, where they dive into their pillows.

EXERCISE 20   Let Your Anger Take a Form of Nature

Here is an idea from Flora Slossen Wuellner in *Prayer and Our Inner Wounds*. Sit with your anger, and see if it might take some form of nature: a bird, animal, waterfall, fire. This example shows some male-female differences. Two persons sat in silence. The woman then reported seeing her anger as the wave of the sea, rising to a crescendo and crashing . . . carrying her feelings into the sea of God's love. In the same moment, the man had pictured his anger as a bolt of lightning, zooming red-hot feelings into the cosmic heart of

God. (I sometimes picture my anger as the grain of sand, irritating the oyster—then transforming into a pearl.) See what emerges for you. Reflect on it; draw it in your journal.

Writing in the Form of Haiku

EXERCISE 21

Still yourself. Then ponder a particular object (like looking through a smudged window onto a pine tree outside) or experience (like seeing Old Faithful for the first time). Play with words using haiku form (five syllables in the first line, seven in the second, and five in the third). Traditionally the second line contains an allusion to nature or springtime.

Writing in the Form of a Sonnet

EXERCISE 22

Writing in the form of a sonnet couples simplicity and complexity, analysis with emotion. Read silently, then read aloud Shakespeare's Sonnet 116.

Let me not to the marriage of true minds
Admit impediments. Love is not love
Which alters when it alteration finds,
Or bends with the remover to remove:
O no! it is an ever-fixed mark
That looks on tempests and is never shaken;
It is the star to every wandering bark,
Whose worth's unknown, although his height be taken.
Love's not Time's fool, though rosy lips and cheeks
Within his bending sickle's compass come:
Love alters not with his brief hours and weeks,
But bears it out even to the edge of doom.
  If this be error and upon me proved,
  I never writ, nor no man ever loved.

The 14 lines are grouped in three quatrains (four lines each) and a concluding couplet (two lines), with a rhyme scheme *abab cdcd efef gg.* This structured poetic form can serve like a picket fence for your garden of thoughts. It can open the gate for more liberated and layered styles of expression. Think of the sonnet like an exercise bar: the discipline returns you to your preferred writing style with the eye sharper and the mind keener. Find a way to share your fledgling sonnet.

EXERCISE 23 — Composing a Prayer in the Form of a Collect

Try writing a prayer in the form of a collect, a simple form in five brief phrases, to give voice to a single longing, to collect your thoughts around one concern. Begin with opening address to the Sacred One (choose a meaningful metaphor or name for God), followed by a descriptive phrase (related to your concern). Then name your request—with a (so) "that" clause to state the purpose. Finally, add a concluding "signature" line (in the name of . . . for the sake of . . . or others). A well-known collect from *The Book of Common Prayer* provides a pattern (I adapted Almighty God using John Coltrane's phrase "a love supreme").

> O Love Supreme,
> to you all hearts are open, all desires known and from you
>   no secrets are hid:
> Cleanse the thoughts of our hearts by the inspiration of
>   your Holy Spirit,
> that we may perfectly love you and worthily magnify your
>   holy Name,
> through Jesus Christ our Lord.

Since the term "collect" originally referred to a collection of people, find a way to share your collect, or try the exercise with a group.

Writing into an Obstacle

For this exercise I suggest putting on a favorite music selection (one without words). Get seated and begin to breathe deeply. Meditate on some obstacle in your life for several minutes. (It can be present or past barrier with a relationship, a working situation, a physical limitation, or financial issues). Begin to write . . . After twenty minutes or so, stop and read what you've written. Give it a conclusion: a prayer poem, or line that gathers up your yearnings as you sit with the situation. Do something else to take a break from your thoughts.

Overnight option: The next morning read over the exercise. Do you find any more insight, some tweak in your imagination? Can you see any way the obstacle opens you to explore something new within yourself, others, or the world? Find a way to converse with someone about insights into the obstacle.

Conversing with Mentors

Drawing from mentors in your life is a powerful way to develop resiliency. **Step 1:** Open your journal to a clean page (or to a new computer document), and set it aside. Pause about five minutes to engage in an "examen" of mentors or mentor figures, living or dead. Savor each; recreate the settings in your imagination. Now begin to enter names of mentors who came to mind. **Step 2:** Set the page aside again; pause to notice an issue going on in your life where you need more light. **Step 3:** Scan over the mentors and choose one you feel drawn to. **Step 4:** Converse with the person using your initials (KIG) for your statements, and likewise your mentor's (JON). Write for about fifteen minutes. Read over what you've written. Highlight or underline responses that lure you or nudge you. Read your conversation to someone, asking for feedback.

Chapter 5

Floating—Focus on Flow

The writing carries you: unity of contemplation and action

Friday Morning

The grandparents were nuts to expect Aguar and Marin to sleep in their last morning. The two had made a pact to get up at 5:39 a.m. to take one last look at the fireball rising over the ocean. Aguar picks up the drum he hasn't touched all week. Feeling its slow rhythm, as Marin holds her journal and watches the tides, she recalls learning (was it from one of the videos or from her science-teacher stepfather?) that your body is about two-thirds water. With Aguar drumming away, it's as if someone whispers her name, "Marin!" Feeling her pulse, she notices her breathing with the ocean's sway. "I just got it!" she proclaims. "I'm two-thirds water so I'm part of the ocean! And I guess the ocean's part of me." Yesterday's diving expeditions have prepared the kids for a slower pace today. Enter Vince and Val: the kids are ready for floating.

In writing this book I have conferred with swimmers who are not writers, with writers who are not swimmers, and with many swimmer writers. All speak with one voice: that the goal of our life is more and more to experience that flow the poet Rilke speaks of—a return to the childlike union of who we are and what we do.

> *May what I do flow from*
> *me like a river,*
> *no forcing and no*
> *holding back,*
> *the way it is with*
> *children.*
>
> —Rainer Maria Rilke
> *Rilke's Book of Hours*

In a spiritual direction training group, one student seemed close to endangering her own well-being, intent to rescue a troubled friend but getting sucked into her friend's despair. A student from Ghana said, "In Africa we tell a story of someone drowning in a river. If you are on the shore and swim out too soon you will get caught in the other's turbulent energies and both will be lost. So you must watch until you see the person just on the point of giving in to the water, and then you can bear that one safely to shore."

Sometimes it takes a crisis to learn to trust ourselves to life; sometimes we are rescued. But if we are wise, we learn to immerse ourselves in awareness, wonder, and practices so that when threatened by the deeps, we have learned the nature of water and can trust life to carry us.

Methods for writing our way into the flow of words can simultaneously become spiritual practices to live into the flow of our unique life with God—our true vocation. Often we begin by floundering our way into those rarified moments when we are carried. To follow their pattern can lead to the constellation of your own

One Thing Necessary, your True North. I pray about everything so I can focus on the One Thing.

> Lord, Keep me doing the One Thing
> while I do the many things.

From Floundering to Floating

In June 1996 my wife and I decided to celebrate our thirtieth wedding anniversary by visiting our son, then in San Francisco and our daughter, then in Los Angeles, and heading south to stay for a few days at Prince of Peace Abbey in Oceanside, California. It would be our first experience at a silent retreat together. In a prayerful atmosphere, I would begin writing a book on men's spirituality, she would read and do handiwork; we would take walks on the beautiful grounds and bathe ourselves in the chanting as well as in the water. I would meet a few times with a Benedictine monk to talk over my writing. The plan worked well.

I returned back East to a full plate of newly forming programs, teaching, and traveling. I never touched the manuscript.

In late October I sequestered myself for a few days in the Jesuit Retreat Center at Wernersville, Pennsylvania. Settling in midafternoon, I told myself to continue the praying *and* writing retreat. I meditated how any nook or cranny can become my portable monk's cell, like Thomas Merton's at Gethsemani, Kentucky. In those moments "Writer's Ascetism," the prayer poem I mentioned earlier, came to me: "Merton-like I hide away, / to pray to write and pray / in this my hermitage, / to birth my heritage: / the gift of the burden, / the burden of the gift."

By late afternoon I was bursting at the seams to open up the document I had begun to write five months earlier. But I was so shocked by what I had written that I had no appetite for supper. It appeared to me as a bunch of dismembered fragments, an irredeemable mess of junk. I closed up the laptop and sat in a sort of nauseous prayer, my unspoken grace before deciding to nibble in the dining hall.

Afterward I took a long evening's walk on the grounds. In the gathering dusk, my path had brought me to a larger-than-life white statue of the Virgin Mary holding Jesus. Collapsing on a bench beneath it, from the hillside I watched the lights as they brightened in the city of Reading below.

Thinking while not thinking about the discouragement of the writing project I had brought with me, at the mosquitoes' urgings I got up to leave. In that moment the thought occurred to me: *there must be at least a few treasures in the junk.* I recalled the story of the boy laughing on his birthday in his room filled with horse manure and saying, "There's got to be a pony in here somewhere!"

On returning to my room, I opened the document and clicked on File: "Save As . . ." and gave it a slightly different title. By this method I had assured myself that my hard-earned junk would still be there if I decided I needed it. But in the morning I would ruthlessly prune everything but a very few budding acorns.

After breakfast I got lost in the pruning process, like stripping excess clothing and being carried by the water. I was finding pithy nuggets of original writing, trashing huge gobs of froth. Suddenly I looked at my watch and it was after 11:30 a.m.—and I would be late for the liturgy in the downstairs chapel. With a huge sigh of thanks, I saved it once more and sprinted to where I heard the singing.

One sentence follows another, is born of the other, and I feel as I see it being born and growing within me, an almost physical rapture.

—André Gide
French novelist

What had happened? Like the drowning African, I had learned to trust my floundering soul to the sustaining power of the Ocean of Love. I was floating. The writing was now carrying me. By afternoon, fresh tides began a cycle of new insights. I was in the flow.

For most of you reading this, such a low-tech method is not new—you have renamed a document many times. But for me each time I click the "Save As . . . " command and begin serious pruning, it becomes a spiritual exercise to remind myself how even the most wretched human being or wasted human experience contains nuggets of grace. In my struggles to release the nuggets, the core of who I am is being pruned, akin to bonsai: not always symmetrical by logical standards but spiritually balanced.

> Bonsai-like,
> this tiny oakling bids me
> to the tilted
> symmetry in the pupil
> of my heart—a balance
> of cleaving,
> leaving,
> and believing
> more than meets
> the eye.

In such ways, can we learn to pray with slick web-sites and frozen computers and text messages as the Celts learned to pray with the rocks and mountains and frozen rivers? If not, are we hopelessly condemned to alienation from our work as Karl Marx claimed?

Flowing and Falling in Love with Words

Youths sat in Saturday morning's sun on the stoop of a breakfast spot in Narberth, Pennsylvania, playing a game of "finish the sentence": insert a word between two finger snaps, two handclaps, and two palms down on thighs. Mathematical and verbal, rhythmic and visual, intra- and inter-personal, kinesthetic and naturalist intelligences were all working while the youth were having fun—in each existential moment. Clearly these kids had fallen in love with words. I'd like them as camp counselors for my grandsons.

From the beginning there were drums, beating out world rhythm—the booming, never-failing tide on the beach; the four seasons, gliding smoothly, one from the other; when the birds come, when they go, the bear hibernating for his winter sleep.

—Jimalee Burton
Indian Heritage, Indian Pride

Falling in love with words and with your subject is 50 percent of getting into the flow of life and love. The other 50 percent is falling in love with the people who ache for you to let them in on your sacred ideas, fears, and dreams. Trust these two oscillating tides to carry you into the Love that will never let you go.

"Listening to basketball sportscaster Marv Albert is like hearing poetry," a friend tells me over lunch. "As a child I felt the same way about Phil Rizzuto calling for the Yankees; the way his voice rose and fell in the twilight seemed like a lullaby." Somewhere they fell in love with words.

At a church auction I bought an antique dictionary stand for a song. Placing on it the unabridged dictionary my wife gave me, we put it in the second floor hallway at the head of the stairs. I hoped our three children would grow up falling in love with words, the origins of words, the meanings of words. I think they did. At the end of a phone call I say, "I love you" and hear back, "I love you." And those three words mean more than all the years of Latin they took or all the books we've exchanged at holidays.

If you're in love, you need simple habits of the heart to pause and keep its joy alive. Small things provide practice studios to rehearse for the One Big Thing. I've discovered two oddly unrelated places to practice being still without impatience or irritation: my computer thesaurus and railroad crossings.

Decades ago I began to long for more public transportation in the United States—as in Europe and Asia—to cut down on cars and pollution and make the world's treasures of employment and education accessible to all people. Along life's way, a young friend Donald traveled by rail with his father and fell in love with trains. It's now his career. When I must stop at a railroad crossing, I let time stand still (while in motion!) and pray for Donald and transportation workers and the world's poor who wait all the time. It's transferred to my writing where I discovered another practice studio.

"Thesaurus" is the Greek word for treasury—a treasure chest of words, synonyms, antonyms, and metaphors. Since I love to use a variety of simple words, I frequently click on my computer's icon and wait for the treasure chest to open. It has become a way to practice the transforming pause. Even if I feel pressured to leave for a meeting or prepare supper for guests, the treasure of waiting to see words on words (like mixed nuts for an appetizer) calls me to a miniature soul feast.

BOOK NEST

I start with Prayer Book's words until
my eyes spot birds gathering winter's
waste to make their nest: seamlessly
book's form yields to poem.

That's how the third day of this praying writing retreat began. I use the form of Morning, Noon, Evening Prayer, and Compline (night) in *The Book of Common Prayer* as a frame for the transparent window of praying and writing. But if, while peeking through the frame, I spy another something Real drawing me, I lay the book aside.

What you don't know until I tell you is that actually I wrote three poems before breakfast, and while tweaking the one above I got so lost in words that the smoke detector pierced my reverie—*Butter's burning in the frying pan!* That's when you know you're writing into and out of the flow of life: the writing carries you. The child in you gets caught in one seamless act of observing, wading, swimming, and diving into streams of words and worlds till you're floating on an Ocean where love and work are one.

Then you get yanked back to the frying pan. But you treasure that lost moment like a keyhole to unlock your one solitary life in solidarity with God and humankind. The Word becomes flesh. You find the words of Torah (the Law of love) are "written not with ink but with the Spirit. . . . not on tablets of stone but on tablets of human hearts" (2 Corinthians 3:2-3). And you spend the rest of your life letting the words out.

I listen to blind pianist Marcus Roberts floating over the keys doing "Maple Leaf Rag"—and Scott Joplin lives again! But beneath his floating keys are years of disciplined intuition. Watch the movie *Ray* and look for that one key scene when young, blind Ray Charles hears the sound of a cricket on the kitchen floor—and his mother doesn't—and you understand the discipline of attention lies beneath everyone who follows his or her bliss to bless the world. You know you're in the flow when you say, *It's been a great morning!*—you've already done a day's work yet your watch says it's only 9:30 a.m.

You practice paying attention 24/7, you wade into writing at least five days a week, and you lay out a fitness program for swimming and diving into it on set days (now it's Sabbath and restores your soul). Then you claim your soul's gift, and schedule stretches for retreat to let your Self be carried into that Ocean of Love.

But if you don't want to end up a drifter, you need a built-in compass to mark your True North. Otherwise,

> *Flow is a state of consciousness in which people feel completely involved in an activity to the point that they lose track of time . . . It is how a writer feels when she is at last able to articulate her most stimulating ideas. It is any time that any of us become so immersed in what we are doing that we forget about everything else.*
>
> —Charles Hooker and Mihaly Csikszentmihalyi
> *Flow, Creativity, and Shared Leadership*

as the Cheshire Cat told Alice, any road will get you there.

Designing Your Life Mission:
Tides of Focus and Freedom

"The surf that distresses the ordinary swimmer produces in the surf-rider the super-joy of going clean through it." In *My Utmost for His Highest*, early YMCA leader Oswald Chambers gives an image for the spiritual aptitude for using resistance. Surfing is sophisticated wading, hugging the shoreline and playing daredevil with waves of insight, wonder, and fear. Surfing is high-risk wading. And your life mission statement is a platform to dive into life's stress to create playful projects for serious purposes.

> *I think it would be well, and proper, and obedient, and pure, to grasp your one necessity and not let it go, to dangle from it limp wherever it takes you. Then even death, where you're going no matter how you live, cannot you part.*
>
> —Annie Dillard
> *Teaching a Stone to Talk*

In the film *Billy Elliot*, Billy falls as he tries to dance. His teacher tells him to keep his eye on a spot on the wall—and it becomes an eloquent dance between focus and freedom. With focus, our cycling around and fallings and risings spiral into a joyous life mission.

"The person with a *why* to live can endure almost any *how*"—almost any circumstances. That's how Viktor Frankl with Nietzche's words distilled the wisdom of survivors in death-dealing concentration camps in his classic book *Man's Search for Meaning*. Jesus said, "If your eye is single, your whole body will be full of light" (Matthew 6:22 AT).

A single focus for your life creates a healing of purpose. It is your unique expression of falling in love with a few words that link you with the Word beating in the heart of the world's chaos. A clear life mission protects you from the undertow and lets you ride and write the waves.

Like the Möbius strip, it has one side yet two. I invite you now to write into your own why to live: "I am here on this earth to . . ." (see exercise 26).

A young man who served in Africa working on peace and justice concerns told me of visiting King Tutankhamen's tomb. He fell into conversation with an elderly security guard on his last day at the job. The guard had been present decades ago, he confided, when grain

> *The place God calls you to is the place where your deep gladness and the world's deep hunger meet.*
>
> —Frederick Buechner
> *Wishful Thinking*

had been found in the tomb—and had taken a few kernels home. He planted the ancient seed, and it produced grain till the present.

The story speaks volumes on many levels. I think of Barbara Kingsolver's essays in *Small Wonder.* She alerts us to how huge agribusinesses export genetically engineered seed to poor countries—seed that doesn't "know" how to endure local droughts—making extinct lower-yielding ancient seed.

But I am telling the story because I believe within each of us is the seed of a unique purpose, just as Lincoln's resolution to make the world a better place acted as an inner compass to turn the tide of his suicidal despair again and again. But when the acorn cracks, how do you discern if the script that unfolds is true to your soul, the Christ-self within you? (See resource 4, Chant: "Listen to Your Soul's Code".)

MIGHTY WHOLE

The oak draws down strength from
the sky, the rain, the sun,
deepening its life in the
Ground of its being,
as at the very
beginning
a tiny
acorn
falling,
lying,
waiting —
then bursting,
breaking, oaking,
lost itself to become
a greater Self in the Mighty Whole.

Testing Your Life Mission: Discerning Life's Choices

Like the grain in King Tut's tomb, an acorn buried in the human soul can contain a miniature Word of Love. Only when an acorn breaks open can it become the oak it is meant to be. If we pay attention, as the soul's acorn cracks it can guide us like the North Star (or the Southern Cross) to stay in the flow of God's leading. Like four points of a compass, we can test a true from a false direction through congruence of inner-outer passion, childhood epiphanies, patterns in our stories, and clues in our dreams.

Each mortal thing does one thing and the same: Deals out that being indoors each one dwells; Selves—goes itself; myself it speaks and spells; Crying What I do is me: for that I came.

—Gerard Manley Hopkins
"Inversnaid"

Inner-outer congruence. "Follow your bliss," Joseph Campbell said over and over. The phrase does not mean, "If it feels good, do it." Rather it is a test to discern a genuine call: *Follow* is a disciple word implying obstacles, pilgrimage. *Your* means your path is unique, no one else's; *bliss* will issue in blessing, not destruction.

Writing can be used for good or evil. Hitler's *Mein Kampf* did not arise from bliss; his cause issued in destruction. A child who can put vicious feelings into words releases the fear beneath the anger. Language frees us from scary things without names so we don't demonize others. Naming the demons in our own fears can change the *daimon* (Greek for demon) from destructive to creative vocational energies. Test specific calls within your mission: look for traces of inner-outer passion where your deep gladness and the world's deep hunger meet.

Childhood epiphanies. One morning little Bruce ran to greet a woman who arrived to do housecleaning. " 'Suffer the little children to come unto me,' Jesus said " (she quoted from the King James Version of the New Testament). *"Suffer" in such a happy moment?* It puzzled his child-size psyche and sent Bruce Manning Metzger on a lifelong dig to update the Bible's language. No wonder he would chair the National Council of Churches' Committee for the Revised Standard Version (1952) and the New Revised Standard Version (1989), opening the Bible's ancient message for the world.

A touchstone to discern between a counterfeit call and a genuine call is to test it with stories and dreams

of one's youth. As a child of seven or eight, Dorothy
Day went into a tirade with her mother, refusing to eat
her doughnut unless she could give doughnuts to the
world's starving children—cracking the acorn of the
Catholic Workers' Movement. I recall at age five I
asked my mother, "When I grow up should I be a minister or a carpenter or a farmer?" I ponder how I'm
doing all three when I write: communicating for love's
sake, constructing houses of meaning, and unearthing
the Ground of Being as I plant seeds of life.

Patterns in stories. Our ancestors charted their course
by the stars and created stories from the shapes of constellations. I wrote in chapter 4 of "patterns in our stories" and their power to shape our lives. The mark of a
life-giving story often involves a downturn into an
impasse followed by an upturn into some fruit born of
the struggle. But the struggle may embody a movement
from the White House to the log cabin as often as the
other way around. A global call to compassion may be
hidden in a tiny tantrum, as with Dorothy Day. Try
connecting your stories to the arc of stories in scripture
and your own spiritual tradition (see exercise 27).

Dreaming awake. We forfeit our dreams for the sake
of others' expectations, a career path, financial stabili-
ty, or wanting to act normal. What is normal? Primal
culture or ours? On the day of Pentecost the apostle
Peter quotes the prophet Joel, "Your youth shall see
visions and your elders shall dream dreams" (Joel
2:28/Acts 2:17 AT). Has Pentecost been repealed?

During lunch break on retreat a woman wrote on
newsprint, "Who's stealing the elders' dreams?" And I

add, who's stealing the visions of our youth? Can we reignite our dreams? Today as I write, the world celebrates the birthday of Martin Luther King Jr., whose "I Have a Dream" speech still calls us to value the content of a person's character beyond class or color. King's vision continues to birth hope for nonviolent actions for peace and justice.

By dreaming awake I mean paying attention to your sleep dreams as friends of the soul that are trying to say, Wake up! I also mean being so alert during waking hours that you pay attention to the sting of a friend's comment, a fantasy you've tried to push aside, a luminous tree by the highway, the distraction of a tailgater—or your dream vocation.

Dreams are signals to wake up to the soul's need for *warnings* (brake lights), *reassurances* (night-lights), and *maintenance* (dash lights). But these three directional signals serve each person's greater quest for the "grail" of life—as in the legend of the Holy Grail: the golden *invitation* and true *vocation* (headlights). Or they point to minicalls within the call, specific invitations for living out your life mission.

All four may intertwine: a frightening warning may be an invitation to action, and the most luminous invitation may frighten us to the bones. To follow an impossible dream, one needs all the reassurances and healthy maintenance available, so as to not go off course. And when you find your golden grail, you drink from it in order to give it to others. Many dismiss or numb what is fearful when it may be the awe of Eternity stirring (see exercise 28).

At age 50, C. S. Lewis had lost his zeal for writing and thought he would be remembered only as a once-famous writer. He started having nightmares about lions. They attacked Lewis's lethargy. Writing feverishly, he published *The Lion, the Witch and the Wardrobe* that same year—quickly followed by six other Narnian stories. The Lion seemed to come out of nowhere.

Paying attention to dreaming can feed your passion and purpose. I've shared my dreams in this book, and I invite you to explore your own (see exercise 28). Living spiritually awake renews physical and mental health, sheds light on relationships with people, and aids in discerning vocational choices that can make the world a better place.

Writing to Mend the Universe: Tikkun Olam

Your life mission becomes a microchip in mending the torn fabric of this string theory cosmos. In kabbalistic Jewish tradition *tikkun olam* means to repair the world. It is a call to healing the universe within oneself and the cosmos. And in Christian scriptures "the ministry of reconciliation" contains twin personal and global dimensions. To be reconciled to God in Christ simultaneously calls us to be agents of reconciliation with neighbors, nations, and nature: nature groans with all humanity in labor pains. Here is the image of giving birth through suffering and struggle.

> This is what one thirsts for, I realize, after the smallness of the day, of work, of details, of intimacy—even of communication, one thirsts for the magnitude and universality of a night full of stars, pouring into one like a fresh tide.
>
> —Anne Morrow Lindbergh
> *Gift from the Sea*

Sexuality and generativity. In the Genesis creation story, the command, "Be fruitful and multiply . . ." is not just about having babies. Fruitfulness in the Bible is a call to bear fruits of love in the personal, familial, vocational, and global spheres of life. Writing creates a healthy way of expressing intimacy and generativity with the world. You conceive an idea; it gestates, you carry it, you may feel sick and weary of holding it, then finally through pain it's released with joy.

Many of my dreams have writing symbols, like this one. *I dream that a wealthy older woman gives me a gold fountain pen. I am a bit self-conscious about using it.*

Reflecting on this dream, I actually drew the fountain pen in my journal, colors and all. Instantly I was stuck by the phallic similarity and symmetry. The dream calls me to use this pen of gold given to me by the old woman (my inner wisdom), but I worry a bit about what people think when I write. To expose my thoughts in writing is a way for me to be generative and intimate with folks I'll never meet. The words flow from the fountain of life.

The dream is still vivid. It came in a time of unbearable discouragement, and even now the dream serves as God's prod for me to keep writing—surely one way my complex sexual-spiritual soul becomes intimate with the world. My ecstasy is palpable whenever anyone tells me how opening texts from my aching, joyous heart creates little patches of healing in the world.

Vocational healing. By now you may be saying all this dream talk is fine, but I don't have the luxury to follow my dreams; I've got to slug it out with one-and-a-half high stress jobs to get myself and my kids through life.

Then I must tell you about Jerry. On the way to Georgia for a conference on Flannery O'Connor's writings, my riding companion had us stop off in North Carolina to visit friends. As we pulled into the driveway she warned me, "Get ready for Jerry to show you his prize albums of poetry written by kids in detention homes."

Within minutes I learned the story: Jerry had been an attorney back in Pennsylvania, but the last ten years it was just no fun. "So Ruthie and I scouted out some halfway houses with troubled youth. I'd get kids writing poetry about their pet peeves and dreams and stuff. By the time we left Lancaster County we were going into half a dozen homes weekly. I endured doing legal work and lived for the weekends. Now we're retired here in Raleigh, and it's taken a long time for children's homes here to open up to us—afraid we were gonna push the Bible. But it's happening now. It's great."

> But yield who will to their separation,
> My object in life is to unite
> My avocation and my vocation
> As my two eyes make one in sight.
>
> —Robert Frost
> "Two Tramps in Mud Time"

The next morning Ruthie told me she went along with Jerry and sat in the hallway and talked with a few women. "But Jerry can get so depressed; I go because he comes back higher than a kite."

Your life mission may await you in the golden thread of your avocation. Guatemalan poet Julia Esquivel was an ordinary schoolteacher in the 1980s when night visions impelled her to write *Threatened by Resurrection*. Poet laureate Ted Kooser and Pulitzer Prize winner Wallace Stevens both had careers in life insurance. Zora Neale Hurston was a professional anthropologist, but when her classic *Their Eyes Were Watching God* was poorly received, she worked as a housekeeper till she died and was buried in an unmarked grave. William Carlos Williams was a pediatrician. The poetry of Japanese orphan Toyhiko Kawagawa was born of sleepless labor as a pastor and political activist on behalf of homeless people. What's the golden thread for you? What seasons your life?

GRIT SEASONING

While I do this grit
work, season
the irksome pieces
with enough
Ahas! to remind me
of the reason.

Intrapersonal healing. Tim's e-mail reads: "As a guy with cancer, I think I would die if I could not write! Does that seem odd? Writing is what is helping me through this." Three or four times a week Tim began to send out missives updating us on his pilgrim's progress or regress. Now that he's doing better, they arrive occasionally.

Crystal Lyde, a student in my class in spiritual direction at Lancaster Theological Seminary wrote: "I've experienced release from the inside out in areas of concern that, if I had not written them out from my heart, I may have never had the doors opened for me to see inside myself."

Your journal can serve like a resident therapist, still in training with the Great Physician. Mining your own exasperations and elations will beckon you to offer your gritty gifts for other somebodies out there.

Interpersonal healing. A mother of small children lay dying of cancer, estranged from her father. Husband and wife co-pastors felt helpless. As a way of praying with her, the woman pastor asked if there were any things she wanted to talk about, offering to take notes. The dying woman whispered a story of childhood abuse by her father. Later she chose to share the notes with her siblings and her mother; they all requested the male pastor to deliver the "letter" to her father. It got very risky; things could blow up. But the pastor delivered the letter to the father. People prayed. What happened the next day the pastors describe as a miracle. The father asked to be reconciled, and the daughter welcomed him as a caretaker for the final days of her life. Mending relationships can be healing even though the body dies.

Environmental and political healing. Transforming afflictive experiences for a social value happens through *sublimation*—which differs radically from *suppression*. Suppression means stuffing your feelings, unawares. Then you detonate—or shrivel. But creative *sublimation* means paying attention to the original pain, emotionally, physically, spiritually. Then you follow an intentional course of action to channel the energies into a creative cause.

MADD (Mothers Against Drunk Driving) exists because victims of car crashes turn their anger for positive changes in public awareness and safety. Julia Esquivel's poetry in *Threatened with Resurrection* became such a threat to the oppressive Guatemalan political system that she had to go to Europe in exile in the 1980s. Gandhi and King understood well this spiritual art of sublimation: their anger at injustice created healing through a lifelong process of social transformation.

Following your life mission can guide why you write, what you write, how you write, and for whom you write.

> Keep this body mending,
> my mind ever bending
> toward the light and lending
> my loaned torch till ending.

Writing and the Tincture of Time

Early in his life, Gerard Manley Hopkins burned all his poetry because his strict Jesuit spiritual director considered it worldly. Later, with a new spiritual director, Hopkins's compromise was never to publish any of his incredible poems until after his death. Hopkins continued to write about light dappled with shadow and pied beauty for generations he would never see.

Van Gogh sold only one painting during his starry night lifetime. Einstein's colleagues thought he wasted the second half of his life because he failed to find one grand unified theory that explained the world of the very small and the universe at large. Einstein died marginalized and a bit pitied. Dag Hammarskjold, secretary general of the United Nations in the 1950s, wrote *Markings* to find spiritual insight for his personal and political path. Years after his death, his path markings still bless the world.

The tincture of time can redeem the rejected dreamchild of your soul: the noble idea or poem or patent or painting or music or manuscript. A lesser soul gives in to sloth, but if you remain faithful to your true Self, you keep rising to express the art of your life. Even if you don't see the fruits in your lifetime, like a squirrel you keep stashing away nuts for the next season or generation.

Love's not Time's Fool

—Shakespeare
Sonnet 116

I gather great courage from witnesses to such vocational resurrections, whether during life or after death.

The tincture of time provides a way of "redeeming the time, because the days are evil"(Ephesians 5:16 [KJV]): it is never too late for any human being's wasted life to be re-deemed, re-valued.

My dictionary tells me *tincture* has associations with healing in the world of medicine. The tincture of time is a powerful image for mending the universe *ad infinitum*. Writing opens a door for a quiet person to exercise power and for a powerful person to express gentleness.

SOLDIERS & LOVERS

The pen that's mightier than
the sword is gentler than the dew.

You lay your words down
in circuits like lovers
to smooch and birth your cause
for freedom, peace, and justice.

You stand your words up
in lines like soldiers
to march into that cause
for freedom, peace, and justice.

You stand them up to march,
you lay them down to love.

Writing with students. The title for Kenneth Koch's amazing book *Rose, Where Did You Get That Red?* came from the pen of a quirky kid, the kind schools have such a hard time reaching. Writing is a bridge for connecting to people with special needs: the sick, the dying, prisoners, adjudicated youth, halfway-house residents.

But this is no do-gooder plan to rehabilitate angry people at arm's length and make them nice. As Jesus tells in the parable of the sheep and the goats at the final judgment, "In as much as you did it to one of the least of these my brothers and sisters, you did it to me" (Matthew 25:31-46 AT). We

Give sorrow words; the grief that does not speak Whispers the o'er-fraught heart and bids it break.

—Shakespeare
Macbeth

meet the Messiah hidden in the lonely, the lost, and the forgotten: we are changed in the encounter (see exercise 29).

Writing with clients. A counselor tells of meeting with a young man who had just lost his father. Toward the end of the session, the therapist told him the Serenity Prayer, made popular by Alcoholics Anonymous. Not knowing the prayer, the man asked his counselor to write it down. Instinctively, the counselor handed him pad and pen to write it for himself. As he wrote, "God, grant me the serenity . . . to accept the things I cannot change . . ." (he began to weep with each phrase), "the courage to change the things I can . . . and grant me the wisdom to know the difference." Writing unlocked the gates of his grief.

The counselor recalled the saying, "The closest way to your feelings is through your fingertips" as he escorted the young man to the door. "Then I ran to the offices of every available therapist to tell the story. It was an Aha! moment for all of us." The experience of writing drew the young man home to his own heart.

Writing for helping professionals. Teachers can gain perspective by writing in the voice of a problem student; a business leader might write an imaginary dialog with a difficult board member or write an unsent letter. Medical residents who learned to craft nuanced stories in a writing workshop said it helped them process their feelings of powerlessness and see their patients as persons, not just medical cases.

A bright pastor, who had contributed insights to the seminar I was leading, got angry at me, and I couldn't understand why. I woke up early and conversed with him in my journal till I heard him say through my fingertips: "It's so frustrating because when I go back to my Kentucky mountain congregation I can't talk about Kierkegaard and Dostoyevsky the way I've been able to do here." Trying to walk in his moccasins changed my attitude with him, and I paid more attention to students' back-home situations.

> *Focusing on the craft of writing . . . provides a means of increasing one's powers of observation and improving one's understanding of both self and others.*
>
> —Anna Reisman, MD
> Yale School of Medicine

Writing for peace. The tincture of time can be concentrated in short life. The late fourteen-year-old poet Mattie J. T. Stepanek tells how he began writing poetry while struggling for his life with a rare form of muscular dystrophy. In his posthumous book *Just Peace,* Mattie describes his first experience of writing poetry: "The words start in the beginning or middle of some feeling or place, and take you to some other feeling or place by the end . . . Poetry is thoughts and feelings chosen into words, combined with sound and spacing chosen onto paper." Poetry is a good way for beginners or professionals to jumpstart our writing.

GIFTED
Sister or Brother
Father, Mother or Other:
May you follow and allow
the acorn script of your creating
heart, given as your birthright,
to unfold into a mighty
oak of peace
which
shields
this tiny
swiftly
tilting
planet
from
self-destructing:
FROM FEARING FEAR ITSELF.

Never Write Alone, Always Write Alone

Sometimes I cry composite tears alone. Sometimes I laugh on behalf of all humanity. What would it mean to live alone *and* all one? Both tides are part of *tikkun olam* — mending the universe.

The more I am alone, the more I realize the mystery that we are all one. Rich and poor, we all breathe the same air. I cannot survive human brokenness without soul friends. By itself a child will die; its muscles atrophy without relationships, touching, holding.

Without the discipline of community, solitude degenerates into isolation and self-absorption; without the discipline of solitude, community degenerates into enmeshment and codependency. Over and over I experience the grace of these twin rhythms.

"Never write alone, always write alone" means without relationships we would die spiritually, intellectually, physically. When I write, I draw from the storehouse of friendships and scribblings over lunch on placemats and Visa-card receipts. I'm writing in community even in solitude. Every book and every poem I read in solitude was written by somebody and was read by many other somebodies. Writing alone I feel close to friends in India and Indiana. Exercise is important too: working out with others in the gym, walking alone around the lake.

My teaching, retreat leading, and spiritual companioning feed my writing. On the fly a fellow professor said to me, "You know the horror story guy's book *On Writing*—ah, what's his name?" "Stephen King," I said. That sent me hunting for my audio version and I "read" it for the third time while driving. Friends would arrive to meet me for spiritual companioning. Some asked, "How's the writing book going?" I'd say, "I'm doing writing as diving and my scuba gear's failing." That often triggered a person's own water or writing story—rejuvenating that person and my resources.

> When I went on a mission trip to Cuba, my fiancée and I made a pact to keep a journal. I'd never kept a journal before. My outward journey sparked our inward journeys.
>
> —Student minister

Closed door and open door.
Throughout his book *On Writing*, Stephen King talks about writing with the door closed (don't think of anyone critiquing what you write) and writing with the door open (think of your sharpest critics as you edit). For me the closed door represents the *via negativa*, the monastic path, the way of withdrawal; the open door

the *via positiva*, the worldly path, the way of engagement. This makes King's image more beautifully complex: the more you interact with the hard knocks of the world the more self-discipline gets inside your bloodstream alone. Besides, sometimes I write with the door ajar: I see who's there and let in only the encouragers. The critics have to go away for a while.

Writing as friendship: C. S. Lewis and Tolkien. In *Tolkien and C. S. Lewis: The Gift of Friendship* Colin Duriez tells how "Tollers" and Lewis created the core of their "Inklings" group—though others like Charles Williams and Dorothy Sayers came and went. Once Lewis and Tolkien agreed to flip a coin: "Let's toss for it, Tollers. Heads, you write about time travel; tails, you try space travel. I'll do the other." It came up heads. Lewis went to work on *Out of the Silent Planet*, but it took Tolkien a major false start and seventeen years to complete *The Lord of the Rings*. Two friends had spawned a writers' group. They shared their written inklings and their inklings of imaginary worlds.

I have a few writer friends who communicate via e-mail or phone, only occasionally in person. For a few months I met with a writers' group and came away thinking, *I'd have rather been writing*. I soon dropped out; not all groups work. E. B. White said it well in *Charlotte's Web* that it's not often someone comes along who is a true friend and a good writer.

For several years I have been a member of a vital Inklings group. All you need is one other writer to birth a small group to read each other's work and sharpen your skills (see resource 3).

Seeing Your Work in Print: Delights and Deceits

What freezes our potential is fear: fear of acting on a long-buried script, fear of encountering brutal realities of the world, fear of yielding to a cause greater than ourselves, fear of dying. I am more concerned to really live before I die.

I have a choice: insulate myself from the chilling realities of life (necessary at times to survive), or learn to walk on water and dance with the tides. Forget the boots, I'll dance to keep warm.

> *Shadow Creek: on my least walk to the mailbox I may find myself knee-deep in its sucking, frigid pools. I must either wear rubber boots, or dance to keep warm.*
>
> —Annie Dillard
> *Pilgrim at Tinker Creek*

I ride my fear of failure and hope for success; each creates energy to keep me in the flow. The Greek *daimon* (demon) represents intense energy that can cripple or empower a person. What is success—getting published? Failure—not getting published? Neither matters if I mine the gift in the process of writing myself through fear into hope.

I dance with rejection and acceptance. The deceit of thinking I'm writing for others acts like a mirage in the desert (even if my work is rejected): it moves me farther along in my soul's sometimes-barren landscape. I picture my work in print and simultaneously release the carrier pigeon of delight. I love it when it comes back with the note, "Accepted." But either delight or despair can morph into the deceitful demons of addiction and envy. For me a simple breath prayer helps: "Lord link (inhaling, hands on chest), I relinquish" (exhaling, hands released). "Submitting" a manuscript is an offering, sacrificing a piece of my life to the Unknown Sea.

I dance with abilities and disabilities. At my first book signing I taped rejection letters to my sliding glass doors to inspire wannabe writers. Some were classy rejections with handwritten notes: "I'm sure your many ideas work well for retreats but do not transfer to print." A friend had said it was lumpy. I mine the gifts in my disabilities.

Ah! The gift: write in such a way that readers feel they're on retreat with me leading them. The disability: my ADHD—nuggets of disconnected ideas. The invitation: capitalize on today's short attention spans (among youth *and* elders) by connecting brief meaningful segments like links in a website of the readers' inner connections. My mission: I am here on this earth to be a link between the Word and the world, a mentor and message that brokenness can morph into blessing for oneself and the universe.

> BRIDGE   WRITING
> I yearn to   pen my Way
> this day to open what I learn
> to bless the cosmos, even under stress,
> to live, and like a flexing bridge, to give
> and sway and dance and link and love at home away.

You can create alternative forms of "publishing." In a dance you use alternating steps—little, big, back, forth, diagonal. "Publish" can mean blogging, e-mailing excerpts to friends, floating ideas at workshops, submitting articles to journals of your own professional groups. Try doggy paddling (an article in your church or organization's newsletter) before long-distance swimming (a book).

One way to discern your call to write is by the noticing the questions people ask. After a meaningful conversation with a younger friend I asked, was he considering writing some of these thoughts? A few months later he said, "You know since you asked me about writing three people in my church have asked me the same thing." When that happens, to use a Quaker phrase, you need to follow your leadings.

I just had an inquiry from a young songwriter, poet, and preacher asking my wisdom on how to get published. My first response was what works for me: some combination of priming the pump myself and grace sneaking in through the back door.

> Courage is "grace under pressure."
>
> —Ernest Hemingway
> interview with Dorothy Parker

Writing as Iconography: "What's in an Image?"

Nowadays "icons" refer to mini-graphics in our computer screens or instruction manuals; they bridge language barriers. Cultural "icons" mirror our fascination with Hollywood-type heroes. In traditional Eastern Orthodox iconography, an "icon" (Greek *ikon*) is "written" (*graphé*) not painted, because the image functions as a visual word. The face of a saint often embodies cryptic details: elongated ears or nose to accentuate listening and sensing; stern eyes to represent keen focus; pursed lips to emphasize few words.

Classic iconography is more surrealistic than realistic, akin to exaggerated characters in a Flannery O'Connor story or a Stephen King novel. Cultural icons—whether Elvis or Madonna—lure us because the melodrama of their charisma and pitfalls mirror our own submerged hopes and hypocrisies. Just as clicking a mini-icon on a computer screen opens up a larger reality, likewise the wildest icons in sports, science, or screenplay can open windows into potential grace or grief.

When I speak of writing as iconography, I mean it needs to jolt the reader (and the writer) into seeing hidden monsters in oneself that may really be angels in disguise, as when Beauty loses her fear by embracing the beast.

Writing as calligraphy (what's the picture?)

"Beautiful writing" (Greek *kalos* + *graphé*) in its many forms calls us to enjoy the art of letters. A friend from China shows me the progression of Chinese characters from the simple early picture to the present-day symbol. For example, the character for water began as three little wavy lines (like a child's sketch) and morphed into the more complex symbol; likewise the characters for a person, sun, and moon.

By contrast, the abstract curlicues on this page contain no

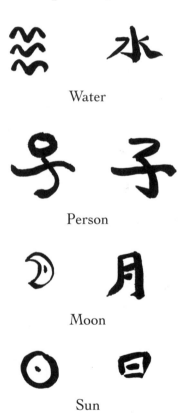

Water

Person

Moon

Sun

such pictures. The best we can do is to use strong images and gestures to evoke pictures in the reader's mind. Or, like seventeenth-century English poet-priest George Herbert, format a poem into the shape of a tree, an altar, or a butterfly.

The Asian practice of calligraphy values the space surrounding the characters as much as the lines. Is this not a call to create silence and space in our writing so the reader may inhabit our word houses? (The popular return to computer graphics and icons bespeaks our craving for visual and emotional connections; witness emoticons ☺ or ☹ in e-mail texts.) In Western culture I wonder what it would look like if we could revive a touch of the tradition of illuminated manuscripts as in ꓔꓧꓰ ꓐꓳꓳꓗ ꓳꓞ ꓗꓰꓡꓡꓢ.

Writing as hagiography (who's a saint?) "Holy writing" (Greek *hagio* + *graphē*) is not about perfect people. Rather, it shows how ordinary people's imperfect lives have helped to make the world more whole *(tikkun olam)*. In *The Saints Among Us*, George H. Gallup and Timothy Jones write about how ordinary people change the world.

Hermann Hesse's classic novel *Siddhartha* makes the fictional Buddha come alive. As Siddhartha he lives in the protective palace of childhood, then gets caught up in the illusions of the world, and eventually comes to himself. In *All Saints*, Robert Ellsberg offers daily reflections on saints and witnesses for our time, including Mary Magdalene, Pope Gregory the Great, Thoreau, Sojourner Truth, Gandhi, and King.

Saints are not perfect humans. But in their own individual fashion they become authentic human beings, endowed with the capacity to awaken that vocation in others.

—Robert Ellsberg
All Saints

In Marilynne Robinson's best-selling *Gilead* we listen in as aging Iowa pastor John Ames writes memoirs to his young son, and we find ourselves painted into the corner of a room filled with mirrors.

Writing as biography (who's a hero?) Once while leading a retreat for an international order of Catholic priests, I invited each to use a journal to converse with a mentor (review exercise 25). More than one came to me to say that an early mentor had in later life let them down. Biography or "life writing" (Greek *bios* + *graphé*) allows you to write about a realistic life and an idealistic life with equanimity. Doris Kearns Goodwin's *Lincoln* and David McCullough's *John Adams* do this masterfully.

For historic fictional biography, look at Alex Haley's classic *Roots: The Saga of an African American Family* or the movie version. Haley set out to write an anthropological study of slavery for academics. Instead, right on your living room sofa you meet his kidnapped Ghanaian ancestor Kunta Kinte in the deadly hold of a ship .

Cultural "icons," like baseball's Sammy Sosa embracing his archrival Mark McGwire, inspire us only to disappoint us. Reportedly, neither could deny using steroids, and Sosa corked his bat to increase power. So F. Scott Fitzgerald could say if you showed him a hero, he could write you a tragedy.

In writing biography, how can we celebrate the heroic act yet also engender transformation in the reader

through the fragile hero's pathos?
Trying your hand at a short story can be
a good way to find out.

Writing as autobiography (who, me?)
Like a classic icon, "self-life writing"
(Greek *auto* + *biographé*) can open a
story window into your living ancestral
wisdom. For example, Kevin attends a
small group of writers and brings his
monthly autobiographical installment
written for an audience of one: his only
child, Sarah. (His colleagues believe he
will someday publish it.) But for now
Kevin's memoir is providing insight,
humor, and healing as he weaves
stories from generations.

> *Otto Rank ... declares that everyone is a hero at birth, where (one) undergoes a tremendous transformation, from the condition of a little water creature living in the realm of amniotic fluid, into an air-breathing mammal which ultimately will be standing.*
>
> —Joseph Campbell
> *The Power of Myth*

Maybe you think you have no ancestral wisdom. Find
the oldest member of your family or your ethnic
group—even somebody on the outs—and ask them for
stories. In high-tech culture, suppertime around the
family table is an endangered species, and so is family
storytelling.

When you penetrate a vein in your story line it
explodes with an Aha!—accompanied by blood, sweat,
and tears. Clarissa Pinkola Estés writes in *Women Who
Run With the Wolves*:

> I hope you will go out and let stories happen to you, and
> that you will work with them, water them with your
> blood and tears and your laughter till they bloom, till
> you yourself burst into bloom. Then you will see what
> medicines they make, and where and when to apply
> them. That is the work.

Gandhi's words "My life is my message" encapsulate the meaning of the Incarnation: the Word becomes flesh. We are back to the Möbius strip, where what you contemplate becomes the message that communicates the self you are in the world. But now you also contemplate your worldly interactions and communicate back to the Christ self within you. Here is the gold: How can contemplation and communication form a seamless process in yourself and the world?

A Summing Up and a Letting Go

Mere observation is never merely observation. If we can learn anything from Werner Heisenberg and quantum physics, it is this: observing an experiment affects the thing observed. Put in reverse: inattentiveness affects the thing not attended.

A newborn child provides a universal example. The response or lack of response of those who observe the child, who hear its crying and cooing, who observe its face and gestures, incrementally changes the child. Conversely, if no one observes the child, the child fails to thrive and dies, even if fed mechanically. Thus all of life is an interactive web.

While my friend taught English as a second language in Rome, a Vatican official invited her to join a small tour down into the *scavi,* excavations deep beneath Saint Peter's Basilica, to walls dating from Rome's founding. Only a limited number were allowed to view the murals because the intensity of human breath would damage the art. For the same reason, in southern France, 17,000-year-old murals in the caves of Lascaux have been completely closed to observation since 1963.

So we return again and again to the power of awareness: tending to one's own self and soul begins a transformation that in turn affects all people and things we see. We move from observation to wading into that ocean of human interconnectedness that flows from the heart of God.

But the tides are so forceful that we can be drawn into a death-dealing tsunami unless we develop skilled methods for navigating the troubled waters. When we do, we may not only avoid the disaster of the Titanic assumption that we are unsinkable but we may also actually discover the opposite: that by giving up omnipotence we may dive into the beauty and the wreckages of life and find the treasure we might have missed had we stayed on the surface.

And wonder of wonders, we find our very selves flowing out of the wounded heart of God through our fingertips into the world's violent transformations and fragile beauty everywhere.

Our knowing by being one with others becomes a steady flow. The more we continue to pray, the less we can avoid getting our feet wet in that ocean of interconnectedness among all persons that flows from the heart of God.

—Ann and Barry Ulanov
Primary Speech

163

Friday Evening

*M*arin hugs a quick good-bye to Aguar, whose mother
will visit from the Philippines next week. As Miguel
arrives, Gram gathers everyone for a prayer of blessing
before she catches her bus back to Kansas. "I want us
together again," says Marin. "Inchala!" replies Lolo, "God
willing." As she traces the sign of the cross on her chest,
Marin's mind kaleidoscopes to the week ahead: tonight she'll
take a shuttle to the airport to meet her mom and fly to
New Orleans. Ah, there they will recognize how water
destroyed people's homes and experience sad happy jazz for
the first time. Back on the plane she'll blink and think of
her Missouri stepsister and float into dreamland again . . .
There they go, rafting down the Mississippi . . . till she
wakens at the Kansas farm pond.

Back at the Beach: Twenty Years Later

*T*he Saturday editorials in the Times of London to
New York to Los Angeles to Tokyo to Manila had
recounted the same saga: Aguar Ibarra had completed his
doctoral dissertation on an original micro-macro electronic
process to scan Vincent Van Gogh and Claude Manet's
brushstrokes, creating a new TechArtTeach program to
train students to paint "after" famous artists. One week
before Aguar's oral exams, a lab assistant pirated and
published the data online. Aguar was immediately
suspended from his Ph.D. program. It had taken two years
to prove the forgery.

Today's Sunday headline reports a wedding at Pennekamp Park on Florida's Key Largo: Marriage of Arts, Technology and Science Makes Comeback: *Aguar Ibarra, the micro-macro digital artist whose TechArtTeach program was pirated two years ago, married Marin Panofsky, his marine biologist partner who discovered a once-thought-to-be extinct coral in a sunken spaceship. Their underwater photographic essays that aired on National Geographic TV are used for training artists, scientists, and educators from Iowa's Waterloo Community College to Paris's Louvre. As the two present their original research, people comment how life comes out of death-dealing stuff. Aguar never got his doctorate.*

Your Life Mission Statement

EXERCISE 26

On a clean page in your journal or a new document in your computer write: *I am here on this earth to . . .* Let your mission statement reflect this two-fold focus: What puts a sparkle in your eyes? (your deep gladness) and What pulls at your heartstrings? (some deep hunger of the world). Avoid being too general (to love everyone) or too specific (to lay bricks). Put your flesh on your mission: "to express love *through* the building blocks of my life, or by creating . . ." For a youth, your mission can guide you for decades to come; for an elder it can flood past decades with meaning. Word it in a way that speaks to employment or retirement or disability. Rework your mission; keep it short; repeat it as a prayer of your heart; put it on a card inside your closet or desk or billfold.

Idea: Reread the opening stem: *I am here on this earth to . . .* Pause for a couple of minutes with this phrase as your heart's prayer, to be present to yourself and God and the world. Begin to write. When you stop, read what you've written once; then a second time highlight or underline phrases that leap out at you. Condense it to one vital sentence. (Incorporate other aspects as goals or objectives.)

Option: Art Your Life Mission. Let an image or metaphor arise that encapsulates the essence of your life mission. Think of a nonlinear way to express it in art . . . poetry . . . music . . . or movement.

Resources: Steven Covey, *Seven Habits of Highly Effective People* (New York: Simon and Schuster, 1990); Richard Bolles, The 2007 *What Color Is Your Parachute?* (Berkeley, Calif.: Ten Speed Press, 2007); and Lori Beth Jones, *The Path* (New York: Hyperion, 1996).

EXERCISE 27 ### Tracing Patterns in Your Life Stories (and God's Story)

Scan over your life to notice ordinary or extraordinary experiences where you have sensed the presence of God: times of plain sailing (my flying a kite on Cape Cod—see page 74) or crisis (my saying something in me would die if I left a conflicted church). Recall particular turning points or key persons who crossed your path (see Psalm 77:11-12). Write your stories or your musings; tell them to someone. Notice if you see a pattern as you look back from your life today. Think of individual experiences as constellations in the night sky: What configuration—a creature or aspect of nature—do they portray? What big story do they want to tell? What pattern do you see in the stories within God's story— the story at the heart of the universe?

Noticing a Dream — or a Daydream

Dreams are a way to listen to our unconscious longings, warnings, and hopes. Active imagination in daydreams or momentary epiphanies have a similar effect. Everyone dreams, though some do not recall their dreams, partly because modern culture doesn't value them ("I had a silly dream last night"). Write out your dreams or draw them in your journal; at the end write "Reflections"—leaving space to muse. Recording dreams amid your day-to-day entries can help you see what's going on that may relate to the dream (though some prefer a separate section for dreams).

Notice dreams of *warning* (brake lights), *reassurance* (night-lights), *maintenance* (dash lights), and dreams of *invitation* or *vocation* (headlights). Note the mood of the dream, names, and places (often they contain puns or clues to some aspect of yourself). Try looking at each dream symbol (car, tree, precocious child) as "part of yourself." Like parables of Jesus, each character or symbol may represent an aspect of your life: for example the buried treasure (part of myself), in a field (part of myself), and the person who for joy (part of myself) sells all (the whole of myself!) to buy the field (see Matthew 13:44).

Resources: Morton Kelsey, *Dreams: A Way to Listen to God* (New York: Paulist Press, 1978) and Robert Johnson, *Inner Work: Using Dreams and Active Imagination for Personal Growth* (San Francisco: HarperSanFrancisco, 1986).

EXERCISE 29 ### Writing with the Least, the Lost, and the Forgotten

This can work with a troubled young person to an older adult. Ask: If you had three things to tell or ask someone (a loved one, a friend, a child, or a complete stranger), what would you say? (Their response may take the form of stories, questions, experiences, suggestions, or advice.) Ask a young person: What are your dreams for yourself? Ask an older adult: What is one of your most treasured experiences? You may get ideas from other exercises: 4 (meditating on an object in the room), 16 (free writing), 24 (writing into an obstacle), or 25 (conversing with mentors).

Options for sick, dying, or infirm: One way of passing on other's experiences is to get their permission to write (or record electronically) as they speak. This is especially helpful for a weak or dying person, for one who can't write, or for one with language barriers. Oral tradition has nurtured humanity's life on the planet through millennia, contrasted to the thin slice of time's written tradition. Coach persons into writing their thoughts and feelings with questions and stories.

The Clearness Committee

EXERCISE 30

The Clearness Committee (originally developed by Quakers to discern readiness for marriage) is a helpful tool for individuals facing a variety of vocational issues. Normally the "focus person," the one seeking clearness, enlists five or six trusted persons (although someone else may suggest the idea) from various contexts of one's life. The focus person writes up his or her situation in advance and circulates it to the group, asking one to serve as convener, another as note taker. (Allow two hours for the meeting.) The convener opens the meeting with silence, then asks the focus person to give a fresh statement of the concern. The convener calls for silence again, then invites discerning questions: "How did that experience guide you?" and observations: "I'm hearing four possible careers . . . " but not "fix-it" advice: "Why don't you? . . . " All happens in a meditative atmosphere. The group may end with a spoken or physical blessing, like clasping right hands with the presenter's hands. The group may be reconvened.

Options: You may include your life mission statement, night dreams or daydreams, and stories in your notes for a Clearness Committee.

Resources: Jan Hoffman, *Clearness Committees and Their Use in Spiritual Discernment* (Philadelphia: Quaker Press of Friends General Conference, 1996), and Patricia Loring, *Spiritual Discernment: The Context and Goal of Clearness Committees* (Wallingford, Penn.: Pendle Hill, 1992). Web: http://www.fgcquaker.org/ao/toolbox/guidelines_for_clearness_committees.htm

WRITING RESOURCES

Keeping a Spiritual Journal

Some people journal creatively with a computer. Others, like myself, find writing longhand taps more primal images and energies, though later I type some journal entries into my computer files. Either way, use your journal to reflect on conversations or events, dreams or scriptures or to create poetry or art (your own or others'). Use pastel colors. Glue things in it: a leaf, a feather, an e-mail note from a friend, a quote or a headline from a magazine. Insert sticky notes generously: jot a fragment of a dream, an insight, or a concern recalled at midday.

I joke about making only two rules. First, date each entry; second, make a mistake in the first one. Trying to say things right is a huge barrier. Another is missed days—so aim for four days out of seven. Probably the biggest barrier to journaling is being too self-critical, writing out of the head instead of the heart. Many of these exercises are designed to link left-brain thinking and right-brain imagination.

Spiderwebbing (or Net Lining) is one such way. You may surprise yourself in relation to an issue where you need clarity. In the center of a page put a word or image of your concern; then create a cluster of thoughts around and below it, branching off like a spiderweb or twigs of a tree. Write or draw free-flow associations,

whatever images or thoughts occur to you (right brain).
Then below it write a prayer, a poem, or an idea in
sentences (left brain), picking up phrases or images you
used in the cluster. Here's an example of the format:

Word or Image

(example: stiff neck)
Written prayer poem picking up ideas from above.

Multiple Intelligences as Spiritual Frames

Howard Gardner's work on "multiple intelligences" offers a holistic lens for "restoring the soul"—passion, integrity, and wholeness in all of life. Some intelligences are highly developed in a person, others less, yet everyone has some aptitude in each. Here is a brief summary in relation to the writing life.

1. *Linguistic/verbal:* Only in relationships do we develop the language of love—oral or written—in words, stories, ideas, or poetry.
2. *Logical/mathematical:* Technological ability organizes reality; theological insight interprets experience; mathematical mystery ignited Pascal's mysticism.
3. *Spatial/visual:* Arrange a room, design buildings; explore geography, cross-cultural events, holy places, and imagination—explore outer and inner space.
4. *Musical/rhythmic:* "One who sings prays twice" (attributed to Augustine of Hippo). Singing or drumming makes the blues beautiful and celebrates life's rhythms in sound or poetry's beat.
5. *Kinesthetic/bodily:* Gestures begin a symphony, decide a baseball game, and express the soul: bowing, kneeling, dancing, handcrafting, or acting.
6. *Interpersonal:* Extroverts tend to encounter the Sacred in community, introverts in small groups or one-to-one; both need genuine relationships.
7. *Intrapersonal:* Solitude, sorely neglected in technological society, nurtures the introvert's joy and preserves the extrovert's sanity.

8. *Naturalist:* The "book of nature" reveals the Sacred in awe and beauty, patterns of devastation and renewal in nature, human nature, and nations.

9. *Existentialist:* Ponder the "why" questions of a philosopher, a scientist, or a two-year-old: Where did we come from? What's it all about? How shall we then live?

Spiritual and emotional intelligences run throughout all nine. For centuries René Descartes' maxim "I think, therefore I am" has skewed modern culture toward printed, logical, technological intelligence. We need primal cultures' richness in the nonverbal areas, and vice versa.

Storytelling participates in all nine modes: witness stories as operas, musicals, ballads, dances, and dramas. A Hassidic story tells of a rebbe, a respected Jewish teacher, who was crippled for years. Struggling to light the first Hanukah candle, he began to tell how his grandfather used to sing and dance. As the old man was telling the story he hobbled on his twisted feet and began singing and dancing. And that is how to tell a story. The body takes the shape of the soul. These intelligences are so usable because they allow the Word to become flesh in every sphere of life. They invite us to learn to yearn, always and all ways.

Writers' Group Guidelines (and Brief Form for Retreat)

Purpose and composition: Four or five participants commit to be present for each other as spiritual companions and writing colleagues (usually meeting monthly).

Sample format: This one is designed for a group of four (with an opening and a half hour for each presenter) for a total of two and a half hours.

- Silence (five minutes; see opening below)

- Personal updating (fifteen minutes; three or four minutes each)

- Writing presentation and feedback (thirty minutes for each presenter)

- Break (five minutes as desired between second or third presenter)
- Process of the meeting and closing (five minutes)

Convener: The convener's role is to open the group with a time of quiet, followed by personal sharing, to remind them of the agreed-upon times and ground rules, and moderate the presentations. (At the end of each meeting choose a convener for the next time.)

Opening: The convener may place an object on a table or stool: a candle, bowl, quill pen, stone, a classic book, or any symbol of writing or nature. Invite the group to five minutes of silence, opening and/or ending the silence with a brief quotation, prayer, scripture, poem, or music—followed by personal updating.

Presentation: Invite one to begin reading (ten to fifteen minutes), call for feedback (ten to fifteen minutes) and when it's close to thirty minutes, create an appropriate transition to the next reader.

Ground Rules: Each person commits to confidentiality and to refrain from advice giving. Beyond these, let the group agree on a format, and evaluate as they go along.

- Listen without interruption as the presenter reads (distribute copies if desired).

- Ask questions; affirm aha! connections; observe unclear areas; suggest alternatives.

- Be comfortable with silences.

- Be attentive to patterns of responses; pause to allow quieter ones to speak.

- Keep the focus on the person presenting (don't switch to your writing).

Process the meeting: End with five minutes to discuss the process of the meeting.

- How well did the group stay focused on the presenter (let each answer)?

- How was the ratio of critique and affirmation?

- How open and prayerful was the group? Were there times it was too fast-paced?

Closure: Find a ritual of closure, let one evolve, or use one the convener suggests.

EXAMPLES (stand if able):

1. Say the Serenity Prayer or other unison prayer or reading (see page 150).
2. Invite each to hold left palm up, right palm down, joining hands, representing each person's receiving (left) and giving (right).
3. Join right hands in center (like spokes in a wheel or a crossroads), then place left hand on the shoulder of the person on your left. Convener may dismiss with a word blessing or encouragement.
4. Pass around a stone, candle, or other object, silently. (VARIATION: This can be done during the meeting as well, using the object like a "talking stick" while the one who has it speaks, then passes it to the next person who speaks.)
5. Bless the person on your right, verbally in a single-sentence blessing—or in silence followed by speaking "Let it be"—the cue for the next person's turn. "Amen" (Hebrew, "Let it be so") can sound strange in modern ears. So I suggest saying, "Let it be" in unison after a spoken prayer or blessing.
6. Join hands and sing the chant, "Listen to Your Soul's Code" (see resource 4).

Retreat setting (limited time): Count off in groups of four for a thirty-minute time frame: Convener: Open (as above) with three to five minutes in silence. Each person has five minutes to read and receive responses (twenty minutes total); process and conclude for five minutes.

Chant: "Listen to Your Soul's Code" RESOURCE 4

Listen to Your Soul's Code

This chant may be sung as a round: allow the recorder to play the 4-bar introduction, and then subsequent voices enter at the 𝄋 every two or four measures. As the voices conclude, the recorder descant may repeat its final two measures as needed until all voices have finished.

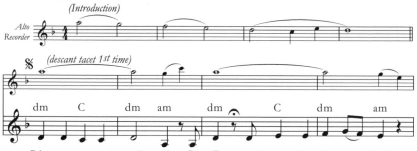

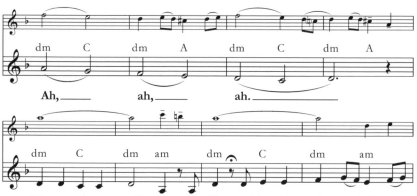

Lyrics ©2006 Kent Ira Groff   Music traditional (arrangement with descant ©2006 David M. Glasgow)

A WRITING
BIBLIOGRAPHY

JOURNALING

*Christina Baldwin, *Life's Companion: Journal Writing as a Spiritual Quest* (New York: Bantam Books, 1991).

Anne Broyles, *Journaling: A Spiritual Journey* (Nashville: Upper Room, 1988).

Dag Hammarskjöld, *Markings* (New York: Alfred E. Knopf, 1964).

Ronald Klug, *How to Keep A Spiritual Journal: A Guide to Journal Keeping for Inner Growth and Personal Discovery* (New York: Bantam Books, 1989).

Thomas Merton, *The Intimate Merton: His Life from His Journals* (San Francisco: HarperSanFrancisco, 1995).

*Henri J. M. Nouwen, *Genesee Diary* (New York: Doubleday, 1976).

Ira Progoff, *At a Journaling Workshop: Writing to Access the Power of the Unconscious and Evoke Creative Ability* (New York: Jeremy P. Tarcher, Inc., 1992).

WRITING AND POETRY

Sheila Bender, ed., *The Writer's Journal: 40 Contemporary Writers and Their Journals* (New York: Bantam/Dell, 1997).

*Julia Cameron, *The Artist's Way: A Spiritual Path to Creativity* (New York: Tarcher Putnam, 1992).

———, *The Right to Write: An Invitation and Initiation into the Writing Life* (New York: Tarcher Putnam, 1998).

* Annie Dillard, *The Writing Life* (New York: Harper Collins, 1990).

———, *For The Time Being* (New York: Viking, 1999).

---

*Highly recommended

Betty Edwards, *Drawing on the Right Side of the Brain* (Los Angeles: Jeremy P. Tarcher, 1989).

*Peter Elbow, *Writing With Power: Techniques for Mastering the Writing Process* (New York: Oxford University Press, 1981).

*John Fox, *Poetic Medicine: The Healing Art of Poem-Making* (New York: Putnam/Tarcher, 1997).

Natalie Goldberg, *Writing Down the Bones* (Boston: Shambhala, 1986).

*Stephen King, *On Writing: A Memoir of the Craft* (New York: Pocket Books-Simon & Schuster, 2000).

Kenneth Koch, *Rose, Where Did You Get That Red?* (New York: Vintage, 1990).

* Anne Lamott, *Bird by Bird: Some Instructions on Writing and Life* (New York: Anchor, 1995).

*Kathleen Norris, *Dakota: A Spiritual Geography* (New York: Houghton Mifflin, 1993).

Flannery O'Connor, *Mystery and Manners* (New York: Farrar, Straus & Giroux, 1969).

Mary Oliver, *House of Light* (Boston: Beacon Press, 1990).

―――, *A Poetry Handbook* (New York: Harcourt Brace & Co., 1994).

Tillie Olsen, *Silences* (New York: Delta/Seymour Lawrence, 1978).

*Parker Palmer, *Let Your Life Speak* (San Francisco: Jossey-Bass, 2000).

*May Sarton, *Journal of a Solitude* (New York: W. W. Norton & Company, 1973).

Dan Wakefield, *The Story of Your Life: Writing a Spiritual Autobiography* (Boston: Beacon, 1990).

*David Whyte, *The Heart Aroused: Poetry and the Preservation of Soul in Corporate America* (New York: Doubleday, 1996).

*William Zinsser, *On Writing Well: The Classic Guide to Writing Nonfiction* (New York: Quill-HarperCollins, 2001).

―――, *Writing About Your Life: A Journey into the Past* (New York: Marlowe & Company, 2005).

N O T E S

CHAPTER 1

10 The Fall 1989 issue of *Parabola: The Magazine of Myth and Tradition* (vol. XIV no. 3) is devoted to "The Tree of Life" in art, mythology, anthropology, archeology, and religion from primal to modern traditions. The Hebrew scriptures begin with a "tree of life" in the middle of the garden of Eden, and feature the fruit-bearing tree as the example of the righteous person (Psalm 1:1-3). Christian scriptures include these and end with the tree of life in middle of the city (Revelation 22:2).

11 Thomas Merton, *The Intimate Merton: His Life from His Journals* (San Francisco: HarperSanFrancisco, 1995), 77.

11 National Public Radio, "Morning Edition," Steve Inskeep interviewing Etgar Keret concerning authors' meeting at Sheikh Hussein Bridge between Israel and Jordan, February 16, 2005.

13 For a summary of Albert Borgmann's ideas related to spirituality, see Richard R. Gaillardetz, *Transforming Our Days: Spirituality, Community and Liturgy in a Technological Culture* (New York: Crossroad, 2000).

14 Thich Nhat Hanh, *Anger* (New York: Riverhead Books, 2001), 18.

14 W. Paul Jones, *The Art of Spiritual Direction: Giving and Receiving Spiritual Guidance* (Nashville: Upper Room Books, 2002), 141.

15 Ester de Wall, *Lost in Wonder: Rediscovering the Spiritual Art of Attentiveness* (Collegeville, Minnesota: Liturgial Press, 2003), 7.

16 Pierre Teilhard de Chardin, *The Divine Milieu* (New York: Harper and Row, 1960).

16 May Sarton, *Plant Dreaming Deep* (New York: W. W. Norton & Company Inc., 1968), 180.

17 Margaret Geller made the remarks about unexpected discovery at Chautauqua Institution, Chautauqua, New York, at the time of her lecture "Expedition Universe," July 14, 2003.

19 Malcolm Gladwell, *The Tipping Point: How Little Things Can Make a Big Difference* (Boston: Little, Brown, and Company, 2000).

19 Robert Frost, *Collected Poems of Robert Frost*, "The Figure a Poem Makes" (Cutchogue, New York: Buccaneer Books, 1986), ii.

20 Betty Edwards, *Drawing on the Right Side of the Brain: A Course in Enhancing Creativity and Artistic Confidence* (Los Angeles: Jeremy Tarcher, Inc., 1989). See also Richard Restak, M.D., *Mozart's Brain and the Fighter Pilot: Unleashing Your Brain's Potential* (New York: Three Rivers Press, 2001), and Robert Ornstein and Richard F. Thompson, *The Amazing Brain*, illustrated by David Macaulay (Boston: Houghton Mifflin Company, 1984).

20 Peter Elbow, *Writing with Power: Techniques for Mastering the Writing Process* (New York: Oxford University Press, 1981), 12.

25 The story of the prodigal son and his older perfectionist brother is found in Luke 15:11-32. For the "neighbor's viewpoint," I am indebted to the late Dr. Thomas Cartwright, former pastor of First United Methodist Church of Hanover, Pennsylvania.

26 Annie Dillard, "Notes for Young Readers" in *Image: A Journal of the Arts and Religion* (Issue 16, Summer 1997), 65.

28 Yo-Yo Ma, interviewed by Gerri Hirshey, "We Are the World" in *Parade: The Sunday Newspaper Magazine* (January 30, 2005), 4.

CHAPTER 2

36 The story of Frederick Douglass learning to read and write is taken from Frederick Douglass's *Narrative of the Life of Frederick Douglass, an American Slave* in *The Classic Slave Narratives*, edited and with an Introduction by Henry Louis Gates Jr. (New York: A Signet Classic, 2002), 364-72. See also Henry Louis Gates Jr., "A Dangerous Literacy: The Legacy of Frederick Douglass" (*New York Times Book Review*, May 28, 1995), 3.

37 Music for "Wade in the Water" can be found in *Lift Every Voice and Sing II: An African American Hymnal* (New York: Church Publishing Incorporated, 1993), 143.

38 *The Gift: Poems by Hafiz the Great Sufi Master*, translated by Daniel Ladinsky (New York: Penguin Compass, 1999), 107.

38 Bruno Bettelheim, *The Uses of Enchantment: The Meaning and Importance of Fairy Tales* (New York: Alfred A. Knopf Inc., 1976).

39 Ashley Montagu, *Growing Young* (New York: McGraw-Hill, 1981), 117.

41 Leonardo is quoted in Richard Restak, M.D., *Mozart's Brain and the Fighter Pilot: Unleashing Your Brain's Potential* (New York: Three Rivers Press, 2001), 180-81.

41, 80 William Blake in *The Complete Poetry and Prose of William Blake*, edited by David V. Erdman, commentary by Harold Bloom (New York: Anchor Books, 1988), 490.

42 For the stories of musicians' and scientists' use of dreams, see R. A. Brown and R. G. Luckcock, "Dreams, Daydreams and Discovery" in *Journal of Chemical Education* (London: vol. 55. No. 11, November, 1978), 694-97.

42 About Werner Heisenberg, see Wayne Muller, *Sabbath* (New York: Bantam Books, 1999), 190.

52 Bill Bryson, *A Short History of Nearly Everything* (New York: Broadway Books, 2003).

52 Betty Smart Carter, "Telling Your Own Story," in *The Christian Century* (June 14, 2005, vol. 122, No. 12), 34.

54 Shawn Wong in *The Writer's Journal*, edited by Sheila Bender (New York: Dell Publishing, 1997), 313.

CHAPTER 3

62 Joseph Conrad, *Heart of Darkness and The Secret Sharer* (New York: Signet Classic, 1950), 86.

67 William Strunk Jr. and E. B. White, *The Elements of Style* (New York: Macmillan Paperbacks, 1962), 17, emphasis added.

69 Lynne Truss, *Eats, Shoots & Leaves* (New York: Penguin Group, 2003). The story is from the back cover.

71 John Fox, *Poetic Medicine: The Healing Art of Poem-Making* (New York: Tarcher/Putnam, 1997), 232-33.

72 Thomas Merton, "Hagia Sophia," in Thomas P. McDonnell, *A Thomas Merton Reader* (New York: Image/Doubleday, 1974, 1989), 506.

72 Jean Giono, *The Man Who Planted Trees* (White River Junction, Vermont, 2005).

79 Thomas Merton, *New Seeds of Contemplation* (New York: New Directions Paperbook, 1972), 14.

79 John H. Timmerman, "In Search of the Great Goodness: The Poetry of Jane Kenyon," in *Perspectives* (May 2003). See also Timmerman's *Jane Kenyon: A Literary Life* (Grand Rapids: Eerdmans 2002).

80 Helen Keller, *Light in My Darkness*, revised and edited by Ray Silverman (West Chester, Pennsylvania: Chrysalis Books, 1994), 21.

80 Trevor Farrell, with his wife and other young adults, were interviewed on public radio Saturday, January 27, 2006.

81   Grenaé D. Dudley and Carlyle Fielding Stewart III, *Sankofa: Celebrations for the African American Church* (Cleveland: United Church Press, 1997), 9.

CHAPTER 4

97   For more on a Christian interpretation of kenosis, see Jürgen Moltmann, *God in Creation: An Ecological Doctrine of Creation* (London: SCM Press, 1985), 86.

100   John Keats, *The Letters of John Keats, Vol. I,* edited by Maurice Buxton Forman (Oxford: Oxford University Press, 1931), 77.

101   *The Shawshank Redemption,* directed by Frank Darabont, 1994 Castle Rock Entertainment: DVD (Burbank, California): 1999 Warner Home Video, a Time Warner Entertainment Company.

102, 106   Andrew Solomon, *The Noonday Demon: An Atlas of Depression* (New York: Scribner, 2001), 15.

105   Joshua Wolf Shenk, *Lincoln's Melancholy: How Depression Challenged a President and Fueled His Greatness* (New York: Houghton Mifflin, 2005), 183.

115   Haiku about a friend who uses a fountain pen composed by Christopher A. Feiss, used by permission.

119   Stephen King, *On Writing: A Memoir of the Craft* (New York: Scribner, 2000), 228.

CHAPTER 5

136   Oswald Chambers, *My Utmost for His Highest* (New York: Dodd, Mead & Company, 1961), 67.

136   Viktor E. Frankl, *Man's Search for Meaning: An Introduction to Logotherapy* (Boston: Beacon Press, 1992), 121. Frankl frequently used this phrase borrowed from Nietzche.

137   See Barbara Kingsolver, *Small Wonder* (New York: HarperCollins Publishers, 2002).

139 Dr. Bruce Manning Metzger told this story in a public
lecture at the Camp Hill Presbyterian Church,
Pennsylvania, shortly after the publication of the New
Revised Standard Version of the Bible in 1989.

140 The fuller story of Dorothy Day can be found in Robert
Coles, *The Spiritual Life of Children* (Boston: Houghton
Mifflin Company, 1990), 326-27.

142 C. S. Lewis story is based on *The Collected Letters of C. S.
Lewis: Volume III: Narnia, Cambridge, and Joy 1950–1963*,
edited by Walter Hooper (San Francisco: HarperSan
Francisco, 2006).

146 The story of the dying woman is adapted from Kent Ira
Groff in *Journeymen: A Spiritual Guide for Men (and for
Women Who Want to Understand Them)* (Nashville: Upper
Room Books, 1999), 77-78.

150 Reuters News (Friday October 20, 2006):
www.yalemedicalgroup.org/news/ymg_reisman.html

151 Mattie J. T. Stepanek with Jimmy Carter, edited by
Jennifer Smith Stepanek (Kansas City: Andrews
McMeel Publishing, 2006), 27.

153 Stephen King, *On Writing: Read by the Author* (New York:
Simon & Schuster Audio, 2000). Stephen King, *On
Writing: A Memoir of the Craft* (New York: Scribner,
2000), 209, 229.

154 Colin Duriez, *Tolkien and C. S. Lewis: The Gift of a
Friendship* (Mahwah, N.J.: Paulist Press, 2003), 100.

158 Chinese Calligraphy by Robert Cheung.

161 For Writing as Autobiography, see "StoryCorps":
http://www.npr.org/templates/story/story.php?storyId=
4516989

161 Clarissa Pinkola Estés, *Women Who Run with the Wolves:
Myths and Stories of the Wild Woman Archetype* (New York:
Ballantine Books, 1992), 464.

169 See Parker Palmer, "The Clearness Committee,"
Weavings, Vol. III (November/December 1988), 37-40.

Resources

173 Howard Gardner in *Frames of Mind: The Theory of Multiple Intelligences* (New York: Basic Books, 1983), 3-277; and *The Unschooled Mind: How Children Think & How Schools Should Teach* (New York: Basic Books, 1991), 10-12. See also *Creating Minds: An Anatomy of Creativity Seen Through the Lives of Freud, Einstein, Picasso, Stravinsky, Eliot, Graham, and Gandhi* (New York: Basic Books, 1993).

174 Story adapted from "A Mitzvah Gives Life," in Rabbi Eugene Labovitz and Dr. Annette Labovitz, *Time for My Soul: A Treasury of Stories for Our Holy Days* (Northvale, N.J.: Jason Aronson, 1987), 240.

Kent Ira Groff, a writer, poet, speaker, and spiritual guide living in Denver, Colorado, describes his work as one beggar showing other beggars where to find bread. He teaches writing workshops at conference centers and seminaries, and mentors other writers. Groff is author of *Active Spirituality: A Guide for Seekers and Ministers, Journeymen: A Spiritual Guide for Men (and for Women Who Want to Understand Them), The Soul of Tomorrow's Church, What Would I Believe If I Didn't Believe Anything? A Handbook for Spiritual Orphans,* and now *Writing Tides: Finding Grace and Growth Through Writing.* He serves as founding mentor of Oasis Ministries for Spiritual Development, Camp Hill, Pennsylvania. As a pilgrim of East and West, he loves to connect with fellow journeyers, learn from them, hear their stories, and write his way into a deeper purpose for life on this out-of-balance planet.